Using Educational Research to Inform Practice

D0143998

Here is a clear, practical and accessible account of the way in which educational research can be used to inform teaching in universities and colleges. The book begins by setting the background to requirements for evidence-informed teaching and then addresses the question of what lecturers need to know in order to become users of research evidence. The authors

- show how the use of educational research evidence impacts on lecturer development;
- explain what lecturers ought to know about educational research;
- clarify the distinction between generic and specific professional knowledge;
- demonstrate how to evaluate the strengths and limitations of research evidence;
- illustrate key research ideas through the examination of case studies;
- examine the idea of good practitioner research and propose how educators can contribute to a knowledge base;
- explore ethical and practical issues in researching in one's own institution.

Using Educational Research to Inform Practice provides the key skills and understandings in thinking about, conducting and applying research evidence to practice in universities and colleges. The use of educational research evidence is now an essential part of HE lecturers' professional development. In addition, the book is designed to appeal to experienced and senior research staff who are engaged in further professional development in relation to course design, quality assurance and strategic development.

Lorraine Foreman-Peck is Research Fellow at Oxford University, Department of Educational Studies and Visiting Professor of Education at Northumbria University.

Christopher Winch is Head of the Department of Education and Professional Studies at King's College, London and Professor of Educational Philosophy and Policy.

Using Educational Research to Inform Practice

A practical guide to practitioner research
in universities and colleges

Lorraine Foreman-Peck and
Christopher Winch

Routledge
Taylor & Francis Group

LONDON AND NEW YORK

First edition published 2010
by Routledge
2 Park Square, Milton Park, Abingdon, Oxon OX14 4RN

Simultaneously published in the USA and Canada
by Routledge
270 Madison Avenue, New York, NY 10016

Routledge is an imprint of the Taylor & Francis Group, an informa business

© 2010 Lorraine Foreman-Peck and Christopher Winch

Typeset in Galliard by
Taylor & Francis Books
Printed and bound in Great Britain by
TJ International Ltd, Padstow, Cornwall

British Library Cataloguing in Publication Data
A catalogue record for this book is available from the British Library

Library of Congress Cataloging-in-Publication Data
Foreman-Peck, Lorraine.
  Using educational research to inform practice : a practical guide to
  practitioner research in universities and colleges / Lorraine Foreman-Peck
  and Christopher Winch. – 1st ed.
    p. cm.
  Includes bibliographical references and index.
  1. College teaching–Research. 2. College teachers–In-service training.
  3. Action research in education. I. Winch, Christopher. II. Title.
  LB2331.F58 2010
378.1'25–dc22   2010001791

ISBN 978-0-415-45009-6 (hbk)
ISBN 978-0-415-45010-2 (pbk)
ISBN 978-0-203-84761-9 (ebk)

We dedicate this book to our families.

Contents

Tables

Acknowledgements

We are grateful to our many students and colleagues, who over the years have contributed to our thinking. In particular we would like to thank those colleagues who commented on various chapters or sections, or otherwise proffered help, namely Liz McDowell, Nicola Reimann, Richard Harris, Chris Rust, Pete Smith, Geoff Hinchliffe, Susan Corr, James Foreman-Peck, Chris Derrington, Kate Hirom, Di Stoncel and Janet Orchard. Their comments have greatly improved the book and their encouragement was invaluable. Needless to say, they are not responsible for any errors, omissions or infelicities.

Chapter 1

What's the use of practitioner research?

Introduction

As lecturers in colleges and universities, we take decisions as a matter of course, yet we are not always aware of their basis. It is only when our expectations are confounded, that we might contemplate how we know that our decisions are the right ones or indeed, what kind of knowledge we draw on in order to justify our approaches. Theories guide our practice, even if we are imperfectly aware of them: sometimes they are adequate, sometimes they are inadequate. We teach in a time when the demands on, and expectations of, college and university lecturers are becoming more demanding, and in ways that we may not all find congenial. Change stimulates responses; and intelligent responses, it is the argument of this book, require careful reflection based wherever possible on available evidence and on a form of inquiry which is often called practitioner research.

Many recent changes have introduced measures of accountability, providing the policy 'drivers' for a nationally assured and accredited schemes of professional training and development for lecturers in colleges and higher education. The Education Reform Act, in 2004, introduced the National Student Survey (2004–9) in order to allow prospective students to compare recently graduated students' views of comparable degree courses at different universities. These measures were no doubt prompted by the introduction of student fees and a concomitant concern that students should be assured of the satisfactory quality of the teaching on offer.

The complexity of the challenges facing lecturers, and the tightening of accountability measures, make an engagement with the development of one's professional role imperative. Not all lecturers will choose to make a career in higher education pedagogy, but all will be expected to reach certain standards of professionalism and to know how to go about using and engaging with pedagogical and professional research evidence, in order to develop their expertise.

The Higher Education Academy has produced a set of standards for the use of Higher Education Institutions (HEIs) in designing their own programmes of professional training and development. They describe what the professional challenges are, or ought to be, starting with the inexperienced member of staff and ending with the very experienced lecturer. The standard descriptors are set out below with the activities, knowledge and values that together comprise the UK Professional Standards Framework for Teaching and Supporting Learning in Higher Education (HEA 2004). The Framework provides common guidance across universities for the content of courses for all staff engaged in supporting the learning of students in higher education, and represents a succinct summary of what is currently expected of lecturers and others who support student learning, in their professional capacity.

Standards – the descriptors

The first standard describes what teaching assistants, lecturers new to higher education with no prior qualification or experience, and those staff whose professional role includes a small range of teaching and learning support activity, are expected to be able to demonstrate at the end of their course.

Standard One

They are required to demonstrate an:

- understanding of the student learning experience through engagement with at least two areas of a possible six areas of activity (see below);
- appropriate core knowledge and professional values;
- ability to engage in practices related to those areas of activity;
- ability to incorporate research, scholarship and/or professional practice into those activities.

Standard Two

The second standard describes those capacities and abilities required by lecturers with a substantive role in learning and teaching to 'enhance the student experience'. They are expected to:

- demonstrate an understanding of the student learning experience through engagement with *all* areas of activity;
- possess core knowledge and professional values;
- possess the ability to engage in practices related to all areas of activity;
- and the ability to incorporate research, scholarship and/or professional practices into those activities.

Standard Three

The third standard is intended for experienced staff who have an established track record in promoting and mentoring colleagues in learning and teaching to enhance the student experience, and asks that the lecturer:

- supports student learning in all areas of activity;
- demonstrates core knowledge and professional values through mentoring and leading individuals and/or teams;
- incorporates research, scholarship and/or professional practice into those activities.

(HEA 2004: 2)

The six areas of activity

In designing courses that meet these standards HEIs are asked to develop learning outcomes that relate to the six areas of activity, core knowledge and professional values which are set out below:

Areas of activity

1 Design and planning of learning activities and/or programmes of study;
2 Teaching and/or supporting student learning;
3 Assessment and giving feedback to learners;
4 Developing effective environments and student support and guidance;
5 Integration of scholarship, research and professional activities with teaching and supporting learning;
6 Evaluation of practice and continuing professional development.

Core knowledge

Knowledge and understanding of:

1 The subject material;
2 Appropriate methods for teaching and learning in the subject area and at the level of the academic programme;
3 How students learn, both generally and in the subject;
4 The use of appropriate learning technologies;
5 Methods for evaluating the effectiveness of teaching;
6 The implications of quality assurance and enhancement for professional practice.

Professional values

1 Respect for individual learners;
2 Commitment to incorporating the process and outcomes of relevant research, scholarship and/or professional practice;
3 Commitment to development of learning communities;
4 Commitment to encouraging participation in higher education, acknowledging diversity and promoting equality of opportunity;
5 Commitment to continuing professional development and evaluation of practice.

(HEA 2004: 3)

The standards have an inclusive structure. The third includes the second, the second includes the first. They are designed so that they follow the natural developmental path of a new tutor where, it is claimed, a concern with teaching methods comes before a concern with student learning, and that concern comes before leading others. In addition all three standards emphasise the incorporation of 'the process and/or outcomes of relevant research and scholarship'.

What the book aims to do

This book directly addresses the requirement expressed in all three standards for experienced and relatively inexperienced lecturers, and others who support student learning, *to incorporate the process and outcomes of relevant research and scholarship into their teaching activities, their core knowledge, and their professional values*. We have concentrated on this element of the three standards since it is an area that is least understood or valued. Indeed, many successful educators do not see the need for teaching and learning to be informed by research or scholarship, except in terms of subject knowledge. We take a directly opposed view. We wish to demonstrate how research and scholarship are relevant to teaching activities, core knowledge and professional values. We therefore advance arguments as well as practical guidance.

The book is of use and interest to new and experienced lecturers and other practitioners with an educational role or interest. The book will be of particular interest to those participating in their universities' Certificate of Higher Education, or Certificate in Academic Practice, more experienced tutors wishing to undertake diploma, masters level study, or professional doctorates and higher education staff developers. Although the book is primarily addressed to practitioners in higher education, it will be of interest to teachers working in the life-long learning sector. Since 2007, teachers in this sector have been required to undertake professional formation. Standards for this sector include a commitment to the improvement of teaching skills through regular evaluation and feedback, and the sharing of good practice with others through reflection, evaluation and the appropriate use of research (Life Long Learning UK 2007).

The book situates the current emphasis on 'evidence informed' practice in its historical context (Chapter 2), explores the nature of lecturers' professionalism and its relationship to research evidence (Chapter 4), and explains what lecturers need to know about educational research, in using and producing research findings (Chapters 3–9). The final chapter discusses four practitioner research case studies which demonstrate a positive contribution to pedagogical knowledge. Chapters 2–9 end with suggested discussion questions or exercises intended to stimulate the readers' thinking about the topics discussed and how they might be applied to their own thinking and contexts.

Our approach

The authors of the book are philosophers of education who are also empirical researchers. They have also spent a part of their professional lives as school teachers.

Many of the problems and debates within further and higher education have been explored at the primary and secondary levels of education. We have therefore, where relevant, drawn on work developed in the context of those educational phases as well as our personal empirical and conceptual research. We have, however, been mindful of the fact that most readers of the book will be from a range of disciplines in higher education, and we have included many examples relevant to further and higher education. Many of the debates and confusions addressed in the book, such as the difference between reflective practice and action research, have been raised by students during the course of our extensive teaching experiences in higher education.

A word about words

Throughout the book the terms 'teacher' and 'educator' are used in a generic sense to refer to anyone with a teaching role in any phase of education. Thus a primary school teacher and a higher education lecturer may both be referred to, at times, as teachers or educators. The phrase 'school teacher' is used to refer specifically to teachers working at primary or secondary level, and 'lecturer' or 'tutor' is used to refer to teachers working in further and higher education. The term 'practitioner' is often used since it encompasses not only teachers and lecturers but others who have a role in supporting learners, such as librarians, academic support staff or managers. 'Practitioner-researcher' is used to refer to anyone engaged in education who is researching their own practice, in whatever capacity. Similarly the phase 'professional role' is used to encompass not only pedagogical matters but managerial and leadership ones as well.

A glossary of terms is provided to aid comprehension for those lecturers new to practitioner research, where the word is not fully explained in the text.

Research, scholarship and the scholarship of teaching and learning

The UK Professional Standards are an endorsement of the idea that practitioners in higher education ought to engage with professionally relevant research and scholarship. Until very recently this would have been interpreted to mean research and/or scholarship exclusively in their subject or discipline area. The requirement to engage with pedagogical research is a contentious one. It is not accepted by everyone that teaching at any level needs to be informed by the use of research evidence in order to be satisfactory. At the heart of this is the feeling that good teachers are enthusiastic experts who communicate their knowledge in an intuitive and spontaneous way. The idea of using evidence seems to negate this positive image of teaching, by imposing a picture of a cold rational approach, a technical rationality, which denies the felt experience of being a committed and enthusiastic teacher. This issue is followed up in more depth in Chapter 4. For now it is sufficient to make two points. We, as advocates of the use of research and research evidence, do not accept that it detracts from spontaneous and committed action. Using research and doing practitioner research does not entail a robotic and inflexible stance in the classroom. Second, while much action and decision making in the classroom is intuitive and spontaneous, it is, or should be preceded and followed by thinking and planning. Planning and reflection are undoubtedly influenced by theories which we may have picked up, casually, from others or we may have read about them and forgotten their source. For better or worse we are influenced by the research and the folklore of others. It seems to us to be a more professional approach to be aware of the theories we are using and to know how to evaluate them. However, although the importance of theorising is obvious, it is another matter to give an account of how research can be deliberately and sensibly utilised.

Nevertheless, the standards in the UK Professional Framework require that lecturers 'integrate', and 'incorporate' the 'process and outcomes' of research and scholarship relevant to their pedagogic and professional roles. As a first step it is important to have a clear picture of what professional knowledge consists of. In Chapter 2, we provide a model and discuss the elements that make up a teacher's knowledge base, which are broadly speaking:

- applied subject knowledge;
- pedagogic knowledge; and
- practical knowledge.

In other chapters (specifically Chapters 3, 5–9) we discuss the skills required to read and evaluate educational research and to engage in practitioner research. Here we examine the ideas of 'research' and 'scholarship' more generally.

Research and scholarship

The Research Assessment Exercise (RAE), which began in the UK in the 1990s, has meant that the term 'research' has an agreed stipulative definition, at least in the UK. 'Research' means original investigation, in order to gain knowledge and understanding. It excludes the merely routine or the development of teaching materials that do not embody original research, but it includes scholarship. The implication is that research must make a new or improved contribution to a body of knowledge, whatever the nature of that knowledge. This is fairly straightforward if we think of subjects such as music or sociology.

'Scholarship' seems to be a vaguer concept. However, the idea of a person *being* a scholar is easier to grasp. We know that this is a person with an in-depth knowledge of a subject. He or she may not engage in research or publication, but will be an expert interpreter of other people's research or work. The RAE defined 'scholarship' as the 'creation, development and maintenance of the intellectual infrastructure of subjects and disciplines' (the full Higher Education Funding Council for England (HEFCE)'s RAE definition of research and scholarship, 2006, is given in the glossary).

Informing the standards descriptors given at the beginning of this chapter is the relatively recent notion of the scholarship of teaching and learning (SoTL). It is proposed that lecturers aspire to the status of scholars, experts in their knowledge of teaching and learning matters, but not necessarily researchers.

However, the general idea that higher education lecturers and practitioners should, as part of their professionalism, incorporate the research of others into their professional knowledge base, is differentially made out by various writers. The term the 'scholarship of teaching', first coined by Boyer (1990) is a term that is not well developed at the moment (Nicholls 2005) and various versions have been suggested.

Trigwell and Shale (2004) for example, drawing on Hutchings and Shulman, (1999) distinguish 'teaching', 'scholarly teaching', and the 'scholarship of teaching'. The first involves simply teaching well, the second involves collecting evidence, using current ideas about teaching, inviting peer collaboration and review and being reflective. The scholarship of teaching on the other hand includes these features but also requires that it is made public and open to critique and evaluation, and is presented in such a way that others can build on it. They argue that scholarly processes involve 'personal, but rigorous, intellectual development, inquiry and action built on values such as honesty, integrity, open-mindedness, scepticism and intellectual humility' (2004: 525). They claim that the scholarship of teaching should be directed to 'how learning has been made possible', an aspect of the activity of teaching (Trigwell and Shale 2004: 525). They argue that the central concern of the scholarship of teaching should be the articulation of 'pedagogic resonance', by which they mean knowledge creation in partnership with students, a concept that, they argue, links teacher knowledge and student learning.

A different approach is suggested by Healey (2003), who, following Cross and Steadman (1996), proposes that it is more useful to speak of the scholarship of teaching as being dependent, or composed of three other types of scholarship originally formulated by Boyer: 'discovery', i.e. research into the nature of learning and teaching; 'integration', i.e. of material from several different disciplines, including textbooks, to understand what is going on in the classroom; and 'application' of what is known about how students learn to the teaching–learning process.

While the notion of the scholarship of teaching has been in use for over a decade, there is no universally shared agreement about what it is or ought to be, and some doubt that it is a useful contribution to our thinking about lecturers' professionalism (Boshier 2009). However, Kreber and Cranton (2000) suggest a useful model of the scholarship of teaching which includes indications of the kind of evidence that would be necessary to claim that one was a scholar of teaching. For example, under 'instructional knowledge' an indicator would be 'keeping a journal or log of methods and materials used'. Under 'pedagogical knowledge', an indicator could be, 'gathering feedback from students on their learning the concepts of the discipline'. Under 'curricular knowledge', an indicator might be 'initiating or joining a committee on program goal review' (2000: 488). Itemising activities that count towards the development of professional knowledge, in key knowledge domains, is a useful exercise. Kreber and Cranton's model, whilst useful for lecturers, staff developers or trainers, does not meet the honorific implications of the RAE definition given earlier as the 'creation, development and maintenance of the intellectual infrastructure of subjects and disciplines'. This suggests that there is a task and achievement sense of 'scholarship' which is causing the confusion noted by Boshier (2009). In other words, the model suggests the kinds of activities involved in the scholarship of teaching, without indicating how one would judge whether someone undertaking these activities was actually successful in pursuing the scholarship of teaching.

However, the present authors are not concerned directly with this wider definition of scholarship activity as set out by Kreber and Cranton (2000). We have concentrated on the development of professionalism through practitioner research, which if done well arguably brings together knowledge of goals or aims, curricular knowledge and pedagogical knowledge. Furthermore, we work with a definition of educational research which was developed in the context of the professional development of school teachers, and transfers unproblematically to the tertiary phase.

Educational research

A commonly accepted definition of educational research, suggested by Bassey (1999), highlights the important point that 'educational research' is always directed at the improvement of policy and practice (either in terms of its effectiveness or its justice), in contradistinction to 'education research' which covers a broader field of inquiry not necessarily aimed at improvement.

> Educational research is critical enquiry aimed at informing educational judgements and decisions in order to improve educational action.
>
> (Bassey 1999)

This book is concerned with educational research in the sense given by Bassey and is developed more fully in Chapters 3, 7 and 8. But for now it is sufficient to point out that 'critical inquiry' involves the study and evaluation of a practice or situation, knowing about others' research on a given topic, and taking action (or suggesting action) which is then (ideally) evaluated.

Educational problems

We argue that higher education lecturers and others should engage with educational research because a research orientation to teaching and learning is needed to solve problems or deficiencies in practice and to explore educationally important issues. The term 'problem' is understood here not as a personal problem, but a problem with our practices, which are constructed by institutions and groups, and are usually common to other practitioners. For example, it could be argued that the assessment of group work, a practice highly pervasive in higher education, is at the moment poorly understood and that this is resulting in serious problems for practice, in terms of fair assessment (e.g. Conway et al. 1993; Magin 2001; Maguire and Edmondson 2001). A case study that amply illustrates this problem is given in Chapter 10.

Suspected deficiencies are, however, not the only motivation we may have. We may have a curiosity about, for example, the characteristics of students who drop out of university, with a view to developing classroom and institutional strategies to support those at risk. On curricular matters, we may be intrigued by the idea of teaching our subject more effectively. For example we may wish to teach philosophy in a way that encourages students to think like professional philosophers (see e.g. MacDonald Ross 2006). These problems will involve us in reflecting on our teaching aims and educational values and in knowing how to evaluate whether we have been successful. As in research in other disciplines, the educational literature is a natural starting point.

It is not implied by this that there is a right way to teach which has been or will be discovered by research. Research informs teaching by suggesting hypotheses or likelihoods, which may or may not work, since students and contexts differ from year to year and place to place.

Stenhouse (1980) made a useful distinction, in this connection, between the study of cases and the study of samples. Stenhouse addressed the problem of teaching an anti-racist course. The problem for the teacher is whether she can be assured that such teaching does in fact work, for it is always possible that it may encourage rather than discourage racism. Research can reveal the characteristics of a sample of schools where it has been successful. The tutor therefore has a basis for judgement about the wisdom of trying it out in her context. However, there are no guarantees, just likelihoods. Stenhouse argues that the tutor should be vigilant and evaluate the effects that her teaching is having.

Another educational example of a problem is reported by Goddard (2005). He reported research that showed that children whose parents are unemployed are far less likely to wish to go to university than those who have a parent who is employed. This survey revealed a pattern that provides a reasonable warrant for a policy intervention for this category of child, given our society's current concern for equality of opportunity to attend university. The study of samples can tell us about regularities in groups or categories of people, of which they may themselves be unaware. However, it does not specify what kind of action is appropriate and it may be that more detailed research with particular individuals (i.e. the study of cases) is necessary in order to gain an insight into the obstacles that such children face and the way in which they think about them.

A case study approach focuses on single instances, such as one student, a class, or even a whole HEI. Qualitative methods are almost always used, since the aim is to gain an in depth understanding of a situation from all the participants' point of view. However, as we have seen with the two examples given above, the study of samples can also provide useful information. Individuals in the wider population who fall into a category (such as students not applying to university), can alert us to problems, the significance and extent of which may be invisible at the micro level.

The two examples above further serve to demonstrate that teaching or policy making are normative activities, and that we can only judge whether an intervention has been successful if it has met our aims and values. Teaching effectiveness, for example, is not simply a matter of increased scores. It is a mistake to think of teaching as a purely technical activity. Teaching methods are always subject to moral judgements. For instance, small group discussion methods are thought to be educationally worthwhile for the kind of learning they help to bring about, such as collaborative problem solving. If they do not 'work', for example with a class that is uncooperative or unduly competitive, the tutor would not be justified in persisting with the method, because educationally valuable ends are not being achieved.

What is practitioner research?

We have given a broad definition of educational research from Bassey above. However, this definition is not enough to characterise what is meant by practitioner research. A useful distinction can be made between 'insider' or 'outsider' researchers (Cochran-Smith and Lytle 1993). Insider researchers are practitioners, such as higher education tutors, nurses, librarians and managers, who research into their own work; work for which they are responsible. Outsider researchers do not typically work (earn money) in the research setting they are researching, for example educational sociologists, educational psychologists, or educational researchers employed elsewhere. Thus educational practitioner research is usually taken to refer to research by people who own and may be a part of the research problem.

We may draw some further distinctions. A practitioner researcher may research her own practice and also be a research user. For example, a practitioner researcher may read the literature about a problem she wishes to research. However, she may simply be a research user in the sense of applying research outcomes or processes, without necessarily engaging in, or writing up a formal evaluation. Indeed, many ideas deriving from the research literature appear in teaching like this. For example, a lecturer may heed the research literature on teaching autistic young adults and produce written instructions for them to follow, since the literature suggests that this aids their comprehension. If the intervention seems to 'work' she may be satisfied, and will probably not wish to evaluate the intervention in a formal sense. Much practitioner research is like this and does not find its way into published outputs, such as journals. However were she to be curious about why it 'worked', she might wish to engage in some more in-depth, possibly publishable research. In the context of award-bearing courses, writing up research is inevitable and raises the questions of research standards and research ethics. These issues are dealt with in Chapters 3, 8 and 9.

Practitioner research is usually small scale and localised to the work setting. However, practitioner researchers may work together, within their HEIs or across HEIs as part of a group endeavour to examine problems that are experienced on all sites. For example, Melrose and Reid carried out a practitioner research project into the development of principles for the assessment of prior learning (APL) across two HEIs in Australia (Melrose and Reid 2000). Research may be carried out with other tutors, or alone, or in collaboration with students. This aspect of practitioner research is explored in more depth in Chapter 7.

Reflective practice and competency based models of professional development

The authors of the Standards Framework did not want to produce a set of competency statements that new lecturers and others in higher education would have to comply with. Rather they were concerned with providing the scaffolding to support the effective tutor and further her development as a 'professionally responsible' teacher, rather than a merely 'professionally accountable' one (McGettrick 2005). This distinction draws attention to two ways of thinking about teaching and professional development. It may be thought of, first, as a set of basic competencies that all teachers must possess in order to achieve a threshold level of effectiveness, for example that they must be able to design a teaching session, conduct a seminar, deliver a lecture, and write assessment criteria. The second way of thinking about teaching goes beyond the description of basic competences to recognise the complexity of the teaching interaction and the obligation the teacher has to meet the learning needs of individual students. Drawing on the work of Schön (1983, 1987) the idea of the reflective practitioner has been seen as offering a better account of what expert teachers actually do. What expert teachers do cannot be completely captured in competency statements because such teachers know more than they can say, or what they do is revealed by their behaviour (Kinsella 2007). As a consequence, teaching is conceived as not simply a matter of being competent but also as being reflective. This means that a process of learning about what is happening in specific classrooms is entered into, imaginative and creative interventions tried out, and evaluative judgements about their effectiveness made. It is easy to see how practitioner research builds on reflective practice in that learning and evaluating become more thorough and systematic, providing a more solid basis for interventions. Reflective practice is further discussed in Chapter 7.

How to read the book and chapter outlines

The book may be read in a linear fashion, in that each chapter follows from the last, and much use is made of cross-referencing. However, for readers more interested in the debates, controversies and philosophical questions pertaining to practitioner research, Chapters 2, 4, 5 and 9 are particularly relevant. For readers more interested in getting their own research off the ground, Chapters 3, 6, 7, 8 and 9 offer practical advice. Chapter 10 may be read at any point. It contains description and commentary of four practitioner research case studies, thus providing illustration for many of the points made in the book and a quick way, if read first, of getting an intuitive grasp of what practitioner research looks like.

Chapter 2, 'Professional knowledge', gives a brief account of how the 'evidence based' requirement in the training standards became established in the UK and explains the controversies surrounding the quality and nature of educational research. The chapter offers a philosophical basis for the possibility of relevant research-derived professional knowledge. An account of the nature and composition of a lecturers' professional knowledge is given, and the case for research literacy concerning professional practice is made.

Chapter 3 asks 'What is educational research anyway?' and explains the difference between education and educational research, and the kind of knowledge produced by each. We consider the purposes that they may serve, and implications for the professional education of teachers. The idea of fixed and flexible research designs is briefly introduced, and three common practitioner research approaches are outlined. The chapter ends with a discussion of quality issues in educational research and a suggested list of quality criteria.

Chapter 4, '"Good practice" and evidence-based teaching' begins by asking what it means to claim that 'evidence should support practice'. This is followed by a discussion of the controversy over the nature of a profession and the status of lecturing as an occupation. Ambiguities in the idea of reflection in the influential reflective practitioner model espoused by Schön and consequent anti-technicist views of professionalism are discussed. A critique of the view that professionalism is distinctively ethical is put forward. We argue that the distinctive characteristics of a professional lecturer is someone who forms professional judgements on the basis of, where relevant, sound evidence.

Chapter 5, 'Handle with care: reading and evaluating research', explains objectivity and subjectivity in research and discusses the factors that are necessary to convince readers of a research report's credibility. The danger of confusing different categories of explanation, and the importance of unambiguous research questions, is illustrated by a critique of learning styles research. Deep and surface learning research is used to illustrate the problem of importing into definitions implied or unsupported preferences. Finally, research into dyslexia is discussed to illustrate the point that research questions in higher education pedagogy require an informed knowledge of empirical work and debates carried out in other disciplines.

In Chapter 6, 'Practitioner research in action: doing one's own research', we note that educational contexts and students do not remain the same from year to year. The sceptic might legitimately ask the question, 'Why bother with educational research or education at all if findings cannot be reliably applied?' Misleading pictures of the way in which education and educational research should be applied are discussed. The idea of 'teaching with research in mind' is proposed. The necessity of adopting an evaluative stance in teaching is argued for, and some time-efficient methods of collecting evidence or data as a practitioner researcher are suggested. The chapter ends with some useful questions that need to be addressed at the planning stage.

Chapter 7, 'Models of practitioner research', defines case study and discusses the most common case study approaches, i.e. educational action research, descriptive educational case study, and educational evaluation as ways of organising one's own research. Action research is distinguished from action learning and Schön's reflective practitioner model. Three models of action research are explained and it is argued that although they may be discrete in theory they are not necessarily discrete in practice.

In Chapter 8, 'Standards in practitioner research' we deal with the issue of the verification of research findings, i.e. the means by which researchers can assure their readers that their research is trustworthy. The notion of validity is discussed in connection with fixed and flexible designs, a distinction that was introduced in Chapter 3. Two worked examples are given of the way in which different ideas about validity might apply in fixed and flexible designs. The former include experimental and quasi-experimental designs, the latter action research and auto/biographical research.

Chapter 9, 'Researching responsibly: the ethics of practitioner research', falls into two parts; the first discusses the ideas of risk and benevolence in relation to practitioner research. The complexity of the ethical considerations involved in quasi-experimental designs are addressed, and a possible way forward is suggested. Some examples are given of non-practitioner research studies that illustrate more generally deficiencies in thinking through the ethical implications for participants and societies. The second part of the chapter gives practical advice on thinking through ethical issues at various stages in practitioner research. It also demonstrates the limitations of codes of ethics and the necessity for ethical deliberation through a discussion of a case study.

Chapter 10, 'Examples of practitioner research case studies', describes and provides commentary on four case studies carried out by lecturers in higher education. They were chosen first because they address important and common practice problems, second because they illustrate different research designs, and third because they all make a contribution to our knowledge of the substantive topic being researched. All four have been published in academic journals. We evaluate not only how well the research has been done, but also what the research tells us about the problems lecturers in higher education face, and how they are related to central pedagogical concerns such as the transfer of learning, the dynamics of collaborative learning, and the validity of certain sorts of assessment.

Further reading

The literature on SoTL is reviewed in Gordon, G., D'Andrea, V., Gosling, D. and Stephani, L. (2003) *Building Capacity for Change: Research on the Scholarship of Teaching*. A Report for HEFCE. Bristol: HEFCE.

A selected bibliography on the scholarship of teaching and learning, by M. Healey at the Centre for Active Learning in Geography, the Environment and Related Disciplines, can be accessed at www.glos.ac.uk/ceal/resources/litreview.cfm (accessed 3.4.08).

References

Bassey, M. (1999) *Case Study Research in Educational Settings*. Buckingham: Open University Press.

Boshier, R. (2009) 'Why is the Scholarship of Teaching and Learning such a Hard Sell?' *Higher Education Research and Development* 28, 1: 1–15.

Boyer, E. L. (1990) *Scholarship Revisited*. Princeton, NJ: Carnegie Foundation for the Advancement of Teaching.

Cochran-Smith, M. and Lytle, S. L. (1993) *Inside Outside: Teacher Research and Knowledge*. New York and London: Teachers College Press.

Conway, R., Kember., D., Sivan, A. and Wu, M. (1993) 'Peer Assessment of an Individual's Contribution to a Group Project'. *Assessment and Evaluation in Higher Education* 18, 1: 45–54.

Cross, K. P. and Steadman, M. H. (1996) *Classroom Research: Implementing the Scholarship of Teaching*. San Francisco: Jossey-Bass.

Goddard, A. (2005) 'Fears of Debt Dampen Dream of a Degree for Children of Unemployed'. *Times Higher Education Supplement*, 20.5.05.

HEA (2004) UK Professional Standards Framework for Teaching and Supporting Learning in Higher Education (updated 8.3.06). Available at: www.heacademy.ac. uk/professional standards.htm (accessed 31.8.07).

Healey, M. (2003) 'The Scholarship of Teaching: Issues around an Evolving Concept'. *Journal on Excellence in College Teaching* 14, 2/3: 5–26.

Hutchings, P. and Shulman, L. (1999) 'The Scholarship of Teaching: New Elaborations, New Developments'. *Change* 31, 5: 10–15.

Kinsella, E. A. (2007) 'Embodied Reflection and the Epistemology of Reflective Practice'. *Journal of the Philosophy of Education* 41, 3: 394–409.

Kreber, C. and Cranton, P. A. (2000) 'Exploring the Scholarship of Teaching'. *The Journal of Higher Education* 71, 4: 476–95.

Life Long Learning UK (2007) New Overarching Professional Standards for Teachers, Tutors and Trainers in the Lifelong Learning Sector. Available at www.lluk. org./documents/professional_standards_for_itts_020.107.pdf (accessed 12.11.09).

MacDonald, R. (2006) 'Learning to Think like a Philosopher: Developing Students' Research Skills in a History of Philosophy Course. A Case Study'. Available at http://prs.heacademy.ac.uk/documents/miscllaneous/researchlink.html (accessed 6.5.08).

McGetrick, B. (2005) *Towards a Framework of Professional Teaching Standards*. March. Bristol: Higher Education Academy ESCalate.

Magin, D. (2001) 'Reciprocity as a Source of Bias in Multiple Peer Assessment of Group Work'. *Studies in Higher Education* 26, 1: 53–63.

Maguire, S. and Edmondson, S. (2001) 'Student Evaluation and Assessment of Group projects'. *Journal of Geography in Higher Education* 25, 2: 209–17.

Melrose, M. and Reid, M. (2000) 'The Daisy Model for Collaborative Action Research: Application to Educational Practice'. *Educational Action Research* 8, 1: 151–65.

National Student Survey (2004–9). Results online. Available at www.unistats.com/ (accessed 1.2.08).

Nicholls, G. (2005) *The Challenge of Scholarship: Rethinking Learning, Teaching and Research*. London: Routledge.

Schön, D. (1983) *The Reflective Practitioner: How Professionals Think in Action*. New York: Basic Books.

——(1987) *Educating the Reflective Practitioner*. San Francisco: Jossey-Bass.

Stenhouse, L. (1980) 'The Study of Samples and the Study of Cases', in J. Rudduck and D. Hopkins (eds) (1995) *Research as the Basis for Teaching: Readings from the Work of Lawrence Stenhouse*. London: Heinemann Educational Books.

Trigwell, K. and Shale, S. (2004) 'Student Learning and the Scholarship of University Teaching'. *Studies in Higher Education* 29 4: 523–36.

Chapter 2

Professional knowledge

In this chapter, we offer a brief history of how evidence-based practice came to be established in British education. We show how a technique that had its origins in a theory of organisational learning came to be adapted to research into teaching within the school system. Thus concern about a knowledge base for teaching and learning in higher education was preceded by a similar concern in the school sector, dating from at least 1970. In the mid-1990s this concern became official and began to be incorporated into government policy on continuing professional development, leading to the introduction of the Masters in Teaching and Learning (MTL) in 2010. Finally, the Higher Education Academy introduced the profession standards for lecturers outlined in Chapter 1.

Practitioner research

We define 'practitioner-based research' as 'research carried out by practitioners into the activity that they are conducting, with a view to understanding that activity and improving it, particularly in relation to their own practice'. Practitioner-based research can be carried out in a range of activities including medicine, law, religion and education. We will concentrate particularly on its place within education, before moving on to practitioner research in teaching in higher education, which is the principal focus of our concern.

First, we need to distinguish between *organisational research* carried out by a school or university and *individual practitioner research*, both of which we understand to be subspecies of *practitioner research*. Although there has been an influential line of work based on Lewin's (1943) theory of organisational development, who proposed *action research* as a way of initiating organisational reform, Lewin saw it as a way of studying the essentials of group life. He advocated a form of experimental methodology. However, action research within the UK education system quite rapidly became the preserve of a very small group of teachers, rather than of educational organisations (Elliott 1988). In fact, it is probably true to say that it is only in the recent present that schools have started to become organisations that actively and competently research their own activity (Cuckle and Broadhead 2003). This is not surprising since organisational research is likely to be complex, sensitive, and to require considerable research expertise. At the time of writing, there is little evidence that universities, at least in the UK, have developed such expertise.

However, this is also true of *individual practitioner research* in higher education, particularly when it involves individuals who have not themselves received appropriate kinds of research training. We use the term 'training' because it is a familiar term in the British context. However, we mean to include more broadly educational and developmental activities within the scope of that term as well. The complexity of this issue was heightened when action research came into prominence in school teaching in the 1960s because of the decentralised nature of the English education system at that time. It was possible, and indeed was a prime objective, that teachers undertaking action research included within their remit the exploration of their own educational aims, curricula and pedagogical practice. Thus normative and empirical activities were both implicated in action research, often in ways that were not terribly easy to distinguish from each other (Elliott 1987). The centralisation of the English education system from 1988 onwards effectively put paid to this kind of research and led to a refocusing of the idea of action research in a more instrumental direction, because of government policy (Elliott 1996).

David Hargreaves' (1996) influential lecture on the analogies between medical and educational research suggested one model. Hargreaves drew attention to the role of practising medical doctors in carrying out research in the context of their professional practice in contrast to teaching, where this was much less apparent. He drew attention to the allegedly poor quality and limited relevance of much educational research carried out in university departments of education and in teacher training institutions, and advocated increased funding of teacher-inspired and -initiated small-scale research projects designed to improve classroom practice.

It was possible to make such recommendations in 1996 because the conditions in which the older form of normative-empirical action research was viable no longer existed. The situation in compulsory education was quite different to the one that existed in higher education. In compulsory education there was a national curriculum, underpinned at least by implicit aims which emphasised achievement in academic subjects, including particularly literacy and numeracy in the primary school. The pedagogical climate had started to shift as well, with post-Plowden child-centred education finding itself increasingly on the defensive although not by any means extinct. Assessment, both summative and formative, had become extremely important in professional terms since the introduction of systematic national assessment at the ages of 7, 11, 14 and 16, and the publication of the results of such assessment. In future, then, action research would be directed to the improvement of classroom practice in conformity with the legislative structure put in place by the Education Acts of 1988 and 1992, the first putting in place a national curriculum and assessment procedure, the second a national system of school and college inspection. Parallel moves on inspection started to take place in the undergraduate part of the HE sector from 1997 onwards.

The Teacher Training Agency (TTA) started to fund action research projects in which teachers were partnered with higher education institutions from 1998 onwards, but the initiative did not develop strong roots and has now receded. One principal reason for this is that it is difficult for research carried out mainly by individual teachers to meet certain criteria of fitness for purpose, in terms of quality of design, methodology and applicability (cf. Hillage et al. 1998 for more on this issue). Indeed, at this time, educational research more generally was coming under assault for its alleged poor quality, most notably in the work of Tooley and Darby (1998), who in a survey of recent research published in leading refereed educational journals, concluded that most failed to meet some or all basic standards of probity in research design, methodology and execution.

Tooley and Darby's study suggests that academic researchers, even those who have some degree of experience and training in research methods, fail to meet threshold quality standards in their research. If true, this also raises a question concerning whether teachers, who usually do not have such training and experience, can realistically carry out research into their own practice that meets threshold quality standards. The TTA's answer, of teaming teachers with academic researchers, would not necessarily overcome this problem if Tooley and Darby's analysis were right. However, their findings suggest a more deep-rooted problem, namely that since the material they surveyed was published in prestigious and highly rated education research journals such as the *British Education Research Journal*, and yet was of poor quality, editorial judgement at the highest levels of the education research community was lacking. Alternatively the possibility was that there is such a dearth of publishable research that editors were obliged, against their better judgement, to publish poor material anyway (see Pring 2000).

It might be said that the standards of probity applied by Tooley and Darby were inappropriate. Since, however, they included the following (Tooley and Darby 1998: 12):

1 the use of triangulation (i.e. checking procedures) to ensure trustworthiness of the research,
2 avoidance of sampling bias,
3 use of primary sources in the literature review, and
4 avoidance of partisanship (ideological bias) in the collection and interpretation of data,

it could be argued that they were merely setting out minimal standards which any empirical research should be able to meet. Their findings were, with few exceptions, however, indignantly rejected within the education research community.

This reaction prompts further reflections. First, some of Tooley and Darby's criteria, although sound in themselves, are nevertheless subject to interpretation. This would be true, for example, of items 4 and possibly 2, if not of 1 and 3. However, it is also possible to argue that item 1 is a requirement that is not always possible or desirable and that a lot depends on how much confidence the reader is asked to place on the conclusions of the research. If, for example, interviews with students are used to generate data which suggest student preference for certain pedagogical methods on the part of lecturers, it is always possible for the researcher to qualify the findings with a proviso that other kinds of data, for example, classroom observation, need also to be collected before firmer conclusions can be drawn. A shortage of time and resources may well limit the range of methods employed, particularly those carried out by one or a small number of individuals (for a good example, see the Chapter 10 discussion of Harstell and Parker (2008). This is why, among other reasons, Hillage et al. (1998), argue for the need for more extensive and replicative studies in the field of education.

However, one line of thought is that educational research should not conform to more traditional canons of scientific research, that the traditional concepts of reliability (replicability) and validity (generalisability) have at best limited application in this field. It is argued that, at its best, educational research should not just be *illuminative* (capable of offering insights) but should also offer knowledge of educational states of affairs. That is, it should give the researcher an insight into the nature of some aspect of education from the point of view of those participating in that practice of education, in such a way as to inform practice, rather than by simply showing how things are (Parlett and Hamilton 1972). At its most extreme the illuminative position holds that fiction is as good a way of accessing educational reality as more traditional scientific methods and even anthropological fieldwork methods (Pring 2000). More radically still, it is often argued that each educational situation is unique and that the most that educational research can hope to do is to depict a particular situation (e.g. Barrow 2005). Lying behind this view is a particular conception of the nature of education as a profession, which we will discuss later in this chapter.

Against scepticism about educational research

It can, then, be seen that not only quality criteria, but also the nature of educational research itself are contested and that such debates have a strong bearing on the nature and possibility of conducting educational research, let alone practical educational research. It may then be necessary to set out a view of these issues in order to provide a rationale for educational practitioners, including lecturers, conducting research into their own practice. In what follows we set out an approach which we believe will address the issues of quality and indicate a way in which valuable research can be carried out.

First of all, we wish to establish a *realist* position, that there are educational states of affairs, which exist independently of whether or not anyone is researching them. We reject *idealist* views, that there is no reality outside the minds of the beholder, researcher or practitioner, as this seems to us to make educational research impossible. This stance does not mean, of course, that educational reality exists independently of whether or not such an institution as education actually exists. In this sense, although educational practices and institutions exist independently of any individual that may be concerned with them, the existence of educational institutions depends on there being a concept and practice of education. To take another example, money depends on the concept and practice of markets and monetary exchange (Searle 1995). Although coins and school buildings may exist whether or not anyone understands what money and education are, the existence of both money and education depend on people understanding what they are and using them. An important corollary is that one cannot understand educational practices without understanding the concepts that constitute them. Second, realism does not entail that there is only one aspect to educational practices. Research may successfully tell us something true about education, without it telling us the whole truth about a practice or an institution. Very often, educational research needs to be qualified in this kind of way.

However, although there are quite a few non-realists in the educational research community, there are even more who are realists but who are sceptical about the possibility of educational *knowledge* rather than of the existence of education as a practice. It is rare to find someone who denies that one can know anything about education; it is much less rare to encounter the view that scientific, or even systematic enquiry cannot tell us anything useful or interesting about it, for reasons that have been rehearsed above. If they are consistent, such sceptics should assert that the claims of educational research are neither true nor false, but this is in fact a difficult position to hold. If someone claims, on the basis of research, that all the 11 year olds in West Dunbartonshire score above their chronological age on the London Reading Test, then it is hard to see how such a statement could be neither true nor false, since an evidential link can be established with the claim. If the claim is false, we know something about the state of reading in West Dunbartonshire, just as we do if it is true. Either way, a proposition about an educational state of affairs, once it is put to the test, gives us knowledge of an aspect of educational reality. Epistemological scepticism about the possibility of educational research does not, therefore appear to be a very attractive option.

We next turn to another controversial issue, the extent to which educational research may or may not inform professional practice. This is a controversial issue because there is an influential current of opinion which denies the relevance of empirical educational theory to professional educational practice. Very often these are the same people who doubt the value of empirical educational research (for more on this, see Carr 2003; Barrow and Foreman-Peck 2005). Strictly speaking, those who doubt the value of empirical educational research for practice should maintain that it is *irrelevant* to practice, rather than false, for as we have seen, to claim that a proposition is false is to claim that its negation is true, thus establishing a potential example of educational knowledge.

While it is relatively easy to show that much educational research is either false or, at best, indicative of a partial truth, it is less easy to show its *irrelevance* to practice if it concerns issues that have a bearing on practice. For example, if one were to read of pedagogical research that claimed that lectures had no utility in helping students to learn, one might be inclined, on reviewing the evidence and arguments, to reject the claim. But a lecturer considering whether or not to conduct a course through the medium of lecturing would be hard put to reject such research because it was *irrelevant* to their practice.

Another line of approach by a lecturer sceptical about whether or not empirical research has anything useful to say to practitioners might be to suggest that common sense – suitably informed, of course, by experience that has been reflected on – should inform professional judgement (see Barrow in Barrow and Foreman-Peck 2005). But this is not really a solution to the problem, since A's version of common sense may differ from B's and common sense may change over time. Until the nineteenth century it was common sense to think that God created the world and living creatures in seven days several thousand years ago. In the early twenty-first century it is common sense in many parts of the world to believe that life evolved as a result of billions of years of natural selection, in which God played no direct role. This example is particularly interesting since there are clearly rival ideas about what is common sense that are still in competition with each other, for instance in the United States of America. Shouldn't we go further and see what the evidence is for holding a belief in natural selection on the one hand and divine creation on the other? After all, if common sense changed and creationism once again became common sense, should we just say 'Ah well, it's now common sense to believe in creationism so that's what we should do.'

We should conclude that we cannot ignore the practice of educational research, even though we may often be justified in ignoring its findings on the grounds that they are false or that their methods of justification in terms of evidence and argumentation are unsatisfactory. However, we need to ask why it is that so many have thought that educational research has little or nothing to contribute to the formation of professional judgement, even when it is well conducted. This is not to say that educational research is not difficult, or that the truths that it reveals are not hard won and often difficult to interpret. These are features of doing it that every serious researcher has to come to terms with. But these arguments should lay to rest the idea that nothing systematic can be known about educational institutions and practices. If we really did know that nothing systematic about education could be known, we would already have established a very significant fact about it – the result of painstaking and systematic educational research. But we know no such thing and no research evidence of any kind supports such a view. What the research evidence does support, however, is the following:

1 Education is a complex and difficult area to research.
2 The findings of educational research that command assent and respect are hard won and relatively restricted, compared to the amount of educational research actually conducted.
3 Many findings are not easily generalised from the areas in which they were generated.

4 Reviews of research have succeeded in validating certain research claims.
5 Findings that are repeatedly corroborated in different settings using different methods are more likely to command assent than those that do not.

If these seem meagre results, then that is partly because of the first point above and partly because there has been a history of over-optimism concerning the ease of establishing conclusions that are both general and express a high degree of certainty. We substantiate this point further in Chapter 5 and show in Chapter 10 that, although it is difficult, it is by no means impossible for lecturers to produce good quality research into their own practice.

What is professional knowledge?

One claim is that teaching is not the kind of activity that requires systematic knowledge of pedagogy in order to be successfully conducted. The claim is that the knowledge that underlies teaching is a form of practical knowledge (Oakeshott 1962), sometimes referred to by the Aristotelian term 'phronesis'. Practical knowledge, which essentially involves our dealing with other people, is difficult to transmit through propositions, being to a large degree unique to the individual who possesses it and difficult to describe rather than to demonstrate. It is acquired through training, exemplification, vicarious example and personal reflection. The media for its transmission are primarily the site of action itself, including the workplace and, secondarily, literature in which illuminating examples of reflection and judgement are illustrated. Teaching like some other occupations, notably perhaps nursing, is an occupation the central core of which is bound up with morally significant interactions with other human beings rather than with the technical properties of materials or artefacts as in, say, engineering or pottery. It is inappropriate, on this view, to apply methods appropriate to such technical occupations to non-technical ones. While it is true that one may benefit from the findings of the sciences of mechanics or ceramics respectively in these occupations, there is no corresponding science of teaching and learning or of caring that can inform teaching and nursing.

Our view is that this claim is false because teaching is an occupation that both requires sensitive judgement based on experience and appropriate moral dispositions but it is also one which can be informed for the better by systematic knowledge about teaching and learning. We will go on to elaborate this claim and to indicate how a teacher or a lecturer may use it and contribute to it.

The idea that teaching involves the putting of research into effect in practical prescriptions is often called 'technical rationality' (Schön 1987) and is widely criticised (Dunne 1993; Carr 2003). This is partly because of the views concerning the possibility and value of educational research that we have already examined above, but partly also because of a view of how research-based theoretical knowledge is put into practice, based on a perception of what is thought to happen in other occupations. Briefly, the view of 'technical knowledge' which

Oakeshott's (1962) work has been very influential in contributing to, is that those activities that involve the drawing on of a body of theory in order to inform practice have to do so via the intermediary of a set of rules that link the theory to the practice. Oakeshott contrasts this kind of knowledge with what he calls 'practical knowledge', about which more below.

Thus, a subject like engineering will draw on a body of systematic research-based knowledge in subjects such as mechanics and materials science. Engineers will have particular objectives in mind, such as the construction of buildings or tunnels. The task then is to match the theoretical propositions to the objective. On the account of technical rationality offered by Oakeshott and Schön, this involves the laying down of rules that link the theory to the objectives by setting down a series of *rules* of action. Even to describe technical rationality in such a way is to illustrate its shortcomings, as there can be no simple rules that link geology and soil science to the objective of constructing a particular tunnel of particular specifications from A to B. It is more plausible to suggest that engineers will move forward with a series of hypotheses concerning route, depth, etc., which will be formed within the constraints of the underlying disciplines of engineering. It is only after repeated investigation and testing that practical prescriptions will be offered and these may well be modified as the project progresses. The whole process of planning may take months as the different parties involved develop the best strategy for tackling the issue. It may well, of course, be the case that some technical operatives will have defined tasks which allow little scope for autonomy and which are largely rule-governed, but such tasks will tend to be for those operatives whose research-based knowledge is limited and who have to rely on simple prescriptions laid down by those whose knowledge is greater. It is a very poor account of the work of a professional engineer or geologist, for example.

The work of such individuals does indeed involve the putting of research-based theory to the service of practical projects, but the process is more complex than this. Research-based knowledge is used, as suggested, to test hypotheses and to form alternative approaches to problems. It involves gaining intimate knowledge of the local conditions, physical and social, of the area in which the project is to be carried out in order to form hypotheses about the best way to approach the objectives within the constraints set out in the project specification, which will include financial and time constraints. After testing, consultation and deliberation these will result in a plan of action which may well be subject to repeated modification as the project progresses, due to unexpected problems that may arise along the way such as changes in geological formation or the presence of water. Occasions may also arise when the engineer or geologist has to conduct their own ad hoc research into local conditions which may well contribute to the underlying theory, in certain conditions. This range and complexity of activities is far more demanding of professional judgement than the recipe-following of the pure form of technical knowledge. Thinking about problems in lecturing can be construed in the same way as thinking about problems in engineering or, indeed, in any other profession.

No doubt a follower of Oakeshott would argue that technical knowledge conceived of as applying rules is only a pure form of what in practice is likely to be a vastly more complex affair in real life. The problem is, though, that in characterising the essential feature of technical knowledge as the following of recipes, no amount of complication of this basic formula can alter that nor transform it into a more complex relationship between theory and practice which involves intimate knowledge of local constraints and conditions. In order to see this more clearly, we need to look at Oakeshott's other category of *practical knowledge*. Practical knowledge is the kind of knowledge which is required in our dealings with other people. It is not underpinned by any theory and cannot be acquired through formal instruction. Its mode of acquisition is, essentially, through interaction with other people, the study of the experiences of others, reflection on it and the development of powers of judgement in complex situations. Politics, for Oakeshott, is a very good example of an area in which such knowledge is required, hence the title of the famous essay 'Rationalism in Politics' (Oakeshott, 1962). There is no reliable theory of politics, and those who try to develop and apply one, such as the French and Russian revolutionaries, go disastrously wrong both in thinking that there is such a theory and in seeking to apply it. Politics is concerned with particular circumstances and particular individuals and courses of action developed to suit the needs of the particular time. Because of the complexity of human life, together with the fact that it is concerned with values as well as facts, it is not possible to formulate anything approaching a theory of politics and any attempts to do so are doomed to fail.

> The modern history of Europe is littered with the projects of the politics of Rationalism. The most sublime of these is, perhaps, that of Robert Owen for a 'world convention to emancipate the human race from ignorance, poverty, division, sin and misery' – so sublime that even a Rationalist (but without much justification) might think it eccentric.
>
> (Oakeshott 1962: 6)

It should now be clear why Oakeshott's views (in one form or another) have become so influential in education. Education is like politics, in that it involves the consideration of values as well as facts and its circumstances are of extreme complexity and vary constantly. There is no well-developed theory of education, just as there is no well-developed theory of politics and attempts to construct one are doomed to failure. If this is true, teaching and lecturing are forms of practical rather than technical knowledge. Although Oakeshott is careful to characterise technical and practical knowledge as ideal types, rarely to be found in their pure forms in reality, it is nevertheless difficult to see how, given the terms in which he describes them, they can be combined in such a way that theory can meaningfully inform practice. Technical knowledge involves the following of prescriptions, practical knowledge negotiation with individuals.

But we have seen that the kinds of technical activities that science-based professions involve do not, except in a marginal way, involve only the following of prescriptions. The use of the underlying theory to construct hypotheses, to construct and modify prescriptions, is far more important. This kind of activity, although it may well and probably does involve more than one person, is not really captured by Oakeshott's descriptions of practical knowledge either, since that is concerned with the development of ends, values and beliefs far more than it is with the acquisition of a desired objective. Engineers working with the client, suppliers, other contractors and inspectors, may well require the resources described as 'practical knowledge' in order to do so successfully, but although their success in this area is intimately related to their technical professional expertise it is not part of it, nor is it part of a continuum of knowledge which stretches from the practical to the technical, at least in the terms that Oakeshott sets out, not least because our dealings with human beings are not, and cannot be, informed by a theory, while our dealings with the rest of the world are and can be.

Our view of professional knowledge

Our view of professional knowledge is that it does not correspond to Oakeshott's characterisation of technical knowledge. The kind of activity that uses technical knowledge in Oakeshott's sense is that of the 'executive technician' someone working at no higher than level 2 in the National Qualification Framework (teachers would normally have level 6 qualifications and lecturers, qualified at doctoral level, level 8). Such an 'executive technician' would be, at best, a semi-skilled worker operating according to set routines which required the rigid following of rules designed by someone else. Even such an individual would also probably require a degree of practical knowledge in order to deal effectively with clients and colleagues.

There is little doubt that teachers and lecturers require a body of knowledge in order to do their job effectively. Obviously they require a sound knowledge of their subject. Since the advent of teacher education and training programmes in the nineteenth century it has been assumed that there is a body of theoretical knowledge to be transmitted that enables them to make use of what is known about how children learn and how to teach them effectively. There has also been a tradition of philosophical reflection on the aims of education, what the content of the curriculum should be and the relationship between teaching, learning and assessment (Carr 2003; Winch and Gingell 2005; Barrow and Woods 2006). The importance of such philosophical reflection on education has waxed and waned over the decades and is now, in institutional terms at least, at a low ebb. Likewise the influence of sociology and history on the theory of teaching has also declined over the last two decades at least. Psychology, on the other hand, has been an important influence since at least the beginning of the twentieth century and continues to hold considerable sway.

There are a number of reasons for this, not least the empirical work on learning and intelligence carried out since the early twentieth century. Likewise the rise of developmental theories to take account of the changing capacities for learning of infants and children, associated with such figures as Piaget, Bruner and Vygotsky, has been highly influential. Although much of this work is philosophical and speculative as well as empirical, there is also no doubt that a large body of empirical work has been carried out which has been used in the construction of theories to explain differences in capacity in learning. Neither should one forget the influence of psychometric theories, particularly of intelligence, on the conduct of education generally (see Gould 1984 for a useful critical survey). Unfortunately, for many if not most of these investigations, speculation and theory building outran the very limited empirical evidence that could be adduced for their claims. Furthermore, the often uncritical way in which the resulting theories were taught and the unproblematic way in which it was assumed that they could be translated into practice has meant that they are regarded with a fair measure of scepticism both within and without the educational community.

However, the position regarding the relationship of educational theory to educational practice is not wholly negative. The very act of refuting overarching theories by falsifying their predictions has itself contributed to our knowledge by eliminating many candidates for our attention. This in turn has led to an interest in less ambitious theory building which is more restricted in scope and more concerned with the more cautious construction of theory (see Howell's study described in Chapter 10). It is also increasingly common to rely on surveys of literature to detect patterns of findings from research carried out at different times and places and in different modes. Individual educationists skilled in interpreting research findings may find it possible to develop a set of underpinning theory that can be put into practice and/or tested in different contexts, sometimes with fruitful practical results (e.g. MacKay 2006). Such trends can be seen, for example, in the research related to the teaching of reading to young children and related research on reading difficulties. It is characteristic of such research and of its application that it is focused on a particular area of learning (for example reading) and that attempts to test such theory have focused on further refinement in practical experiments to validate the theory in the context of improving school performance (Bryant and Bradley 1985; Watson and Johnston 1999; MacKay 2006).

Research and professional knowledge in teaching

It is useful to distinguish the different kinds of knowledge that teachers and lecturers are said to have. This will allow us to identify where theory and research have a role and where the personal research of lecturers into their own practice can play a role.

Subject knowledge

No-one disputes that teachers who have a body of propositional knowledge to impart need to possess that knowledge themselves, up to and beyond the level at which they intend to teach it. Although this is a very important part of a lecturer's knowledge and although it is more complex than the mere transmission of propositions, we will say no more about it in general terms here.

Applied subject knowledge

This is described as the subject knowledge necessary to organise the effective teaching of the main body of subject knowledge. It is an area in which practitioners can make a contribution. It will include such features as understanding of the progression of conceptual connections and conceptual complexity within a subject with a view to ordering it in a pedagogically effective way. As such it overlaps with the next category that we will consider.

Pedagogic knowledge

Pedagogic knowledge is knowledge of effective methods of teaching and learning. It is usually considered to contain general elements, for example, general propositions about how adults learn effectively, with applied subject knowledge about how they learn effectively in particular subject areas (see above). The critical question for us is the extent to which such knowledge is ever capable of being formed into a theory and, if so, how general and context independent such a theory could possibly be (see Solon 2007, which we discuss in Chapter 10).

Practical knowledge of how to teach

Everyone agrees that teaching is a practical activity. Disagreement occurs as to whether or not it needs to be informed by non-subject knowledge. Few would disagree that applied subject knowledge is at least implicitly used in teaching, but more would question whether or not it is used explicitly, as opposed to being drawn on tacitly during the course of teaching. More generally, it is often claimed that knowledge of how to teach is akin to practical knowledge in Oakeshott's sense. This claim, if true, largely precludes any role for pedagogical theory in its formation. We maintain, however, that it can be effectively researched – see Chapter 10 for examples.

We have already argued for two propositions:

1   Pedagogical theory is not very well-developed.
2   Its use is unavoidable in the practical knowledge of teaching.

The point that can still be disputed, however, is whether or not pedagogical theory, such as it is, should be consciously deployed in the activity of teaching, or whether it is sufficient for it to 'run in the background' as a set of implicit constraints on certain kinds of approach to teaching. One obvious worry with the former approach is that it appears to involve 'technical knowledge' in Oakeshott's sense and thus the rigid deployment of pedagogical recipes in contexts and forms that are often inappropriate to the situations in which lecturers find themselves. We have already dealt with this objection by pointing out that engagement with theory can involve interpretation and adaptation of theoretical claims to the particular demands of teaching. Indeed, it is hard to see how lecturers, if they were to adopt some theory as a basis for their practice, could do otherwise and at the same time hope to use that theoretical basis in a fruitful way.

It seems to us that the problem of using research in teaching and lecturing does not lie only in the general claim that effective teaching and lecturing requires some theoretical knowledge concerning how to teach a particular subject and general propositions about how adults learn. It is also concerned with how one is to describe the putting of that knowledge into practice. Given the undeveloped, context dependent and disaggregated nature of knowledge about learning, the answer to this question is not likely to be straightforward. In concluding this chapter we make several claims about the relation of the theory of education to practice and look forward to the role of lecturers in making a contribution to that knowledge.

Critique of theory

The first claim is that lecturers should adopt a critical attitude to pedagogic theory just as they would to any other claim that they come across in their academic work. It is not the role of lecturers to take pedagogical theory on trust without good warrant.

In order to do this some conditions should be met.

Normative theory of education

Like any other subject, education has a conceptual structure into which are organised the various categories for thinking about the subject, notably aims, curriculum, pedagogy and assessment (Winch 1996). The relationships between these central organising concepts are often disputed and this is particularly the case concerning the relationship between pedagogy and assessment. Lecturers need to be familiar with these broad concepts and how they are thought to relate to each other. In addition, they need to work out their own positions on what the aims of their work are, the proper structure of the curriculum and the ethical parameters of pedagogical and assessment practice. Even if they are not in a position to implement all their values, they can thus at least know where they stand in relation to them.

Knowledge of methodology

Education is a discipline that makes use of a very wide variety of methodologies, both empirical and conceptual. One would expect lecturers to have some acquaintance with the broad outlines of these methodologies to the extent that they can comment critically on the evidence and arguments produced for claims. There are published canons for threshold standards of probity in educational research (e.g. Tooley and Darby 1998) which can serve as a starting point when evaluating the suitability and quality of application of methodologies. In any case, evaluation of research presupposes some acquaintance with the methodological principles by which it has been conducted. It should be noted that the methodologies employed in educational research may differ in significant ways from those employed in the lecturer's subject discipline and may need further study in order to deepen acquaintance.

Interpretation of theory in practical situations

Corroboration, yet alone confirmation, of theoretical predictions presupposes that they be subject to testing in a variety of conditions. But before that can be done the testing situation needs to be evaluated for its appropriateness for the application of a particular theory, and this may not always be a straightforward matter. The complexity of social situations in general and educational ones in particular make the number of relevant variables in play considerable, and the interaction of these relevant variables with each other needs to be taken into account when applying theory to practice.

Application of theory and reflexive contribution

The application of a theory or approach derived from a theory will often lead to unexpected results or to results that have poor corroborative value for the theory in question. Interpretation after the fact of why this might be so can be a complex matter and may well involve the factors already considered above. Such after the fact interpretation can also be very important in further theory development, as it may shed light on contextual factors that limit or otherwise affect the scope of application of theoretical positions, or may prompt extension or further refinement of the theory. More formally, the application of a theory to a practical situation can lead to the testing of hypotheses and thus contribute to theory development.

The ability to operate in these four modes is what we call *research literacy* in one's own professional practice. The conditions will be considered in more detail throughout the book. Our argument is, however, that research literacy is a condition of a sound professional approach to teaching in higher education for reasons that we will summarise.

- It is desirable to use approaches that are coherent and fit one's values about teaching.
- It is necessary to take critical account of theories, both normative and empirical, about how lecturing and teaching should be done.

- It is essential to subject even well corroborated approaches to practical trial in order to learn the conditions in which they may or may not be effective.
- It is essential to advance pedagogical knowledge through the trialling of innovation in pedagogical settings.

Exercises

1 'Research evidence is irrelevant to teaching in higher education.' Do you agree? What arguments support your point of view?
2 The idea of technical rationality is a misleading way of characterising the way in which evidence gets into practice. Defend this view.
3 Suppose you were invited to an interview for a position as a lecturer in a university or college. How would you answer questions about:

- Your subject knowledge;
- Your applied subject knowledge;
- Your pedagogic knowledge;
- Your practical knowledge of how to teach.

And your normative theory of education?

References

Barrow, R. (2005) 'The Case Against Empirical Research in Education', in R. Barrow and L. Foreman-Peck, *What Use Is Educational Research? A Debate*. London: Philosophy of Education Society of Great Britain.

Barrow, R. and Woods, R. (2006) *An Introduction to Philosophy of Education*. 3rd edn. London: Routledge.

Bryant, M. and Bradley, L. (1985) *Children's Reading Problems*. London: Methuen.

Carr, D. (2003) *Making Sense of Education*. London: Routledge.

Cuckle, P. and Broadhead, P. (2003) 'Developments in Development Planning in English Primary Schools: 1994–2001'. *School Leadership and Management* 23, 2: 229–40.

Dunne, J. (1993) *Back to the Rough Ground*. Chicago: University of Notre Dame Press.

Elliott, J. (1987) 'Educational Theory, Practical Philosophy and Action Research'. *British Journal of Educational Studies* XXXV, 2: 149–70.

——(1988) 'Teachers as Researchers', in J. P. Keeves (ed.) Educational Research, Methodology and Measurement: An International Handbook (pp. 78–81). London: Pergamon Press.

——(1996) 'School Effectiveness Research and Its Critics: Alternative Visions of Schooling'. *Cambridge Journal of Education* 26, 2: 199–224.

Gould, S. J. (1984) *The Mismeasurement of Man*. London: Penguin.

Hargreaves, D. (1996) 'Teaching as a Research-Based Profession: Possibilities and Prospects'. TTA Annual Lecture, 1996.

Hartsell, B. D. and Parker, A. J. (2008) 'Evaluation of Problem-Based Learning as a Method for Teaching Social Work Administration: A Content Analysis'. *Administration in Social Work* 32, 3: 44–62.

Hillage, J., Pearson, R., Anderson, A. and Tamkin, P. (1998) *Excellence in Research on Schools*. London: DfEE.

Lewin, K. (1943). 'Psychological Ecology', in D. Cartwright (ed.) *Field Theory in Social Science* (pp. 170–87). New York: Harper and Row.

MacKay, T. (2006) *The West Dunbartonshire Literacy Initiative*. West Dunbartonshire Council.

Oakeshott, M. (1962) *Rationalism in Politics*. London: Methuen.

Parlett, M. and Hamilton, D. (1972) 'Evaluation as Illumination: A New Approach to the Study of Innovatory Programmes', republished in M. Parlett and G. Dearden (eds) (1977) *Introduction to Illuminative Evaluation: Studies in Higher Education*. Cardiff-by-the-Sea, CA, USA: Pacific Soundings Press/Guildford: Society for Research into Higher Education.

Pring, R. (2000) 'Editorial: Educational Research'. *British Journal of Educational Studies* 48, 1: 1–9.

Schön, D. (1987) *Educating the Reflective Practitioner*. San Francisco: Jossey-Bass.

——(1991) *The Reflective Practitioner: How Professionals Think in Action*. Aldershot: Avebury.

Searle, J. (1995) *The Construction of Social Reality*. London: Penguin.

Smith, R. (2007) 'Proteus Rising: Re-imagining Educational Research'. Annual Conference of the Philosophy of Education Society of Great Britain, Oxford, April.

Solon, T. (2007) 'Generic Critical Thinking Infusion and Course Content Learning in Introductory Psychology'. *Journal of Instructional Psychology* 34, 2: 95–109.

Tooley, J. and Darby, D. (1998) *Educational Research: A Critique*. London: OFSTED.

Watson, J. and Johnston, R. (1999) *Accelerating Reading Achievement: The Effectiveness of Synthetic Phonics*. www.scotland.gov.uk/library/documents7/interchg.pdf.

Winch, C. (1996) *Quality and Education*. London: Blackwell.

Winch, C. and Gingell, J. (2005) *Philosophy and Educational Policy: A Critical Introduction*. London: Routledge.

Chapter 3

What is educational research anyway?

Introduction: educational and education research

We argued in Chapter 2 that engaging in research and using research findings have a part to play in a lecturer's professionalism. In this chapter we introduce some distinctions originally developed for teachers working in the primary and secondary sectors of education which have been usefully applied to the tertiary sector.

A central distinction is between education and educational research. We examine this distinction drawing on the influential work of Elliott (2007) and argue that while it is useful for thinking about the distinctive nature of practitioner research, it should not be thought of as a categorical distinction, or to imply a value judgement, at least on our part, about the superiority of one form of research over another.

Elliott characterised 'education research' as research *on or about* education and 'educational research' as research *for* education (Elliott 1978). He argued that practitioners, i.e. lecturers and other educators, were engaged in the latter. In drawing this contrast, he was pointing to major differences between two sorts of research endeavour. For instance, the former is 'scientific', employing technical or theoretical terms; the latter is based on common sense understandings. The former seeks law-like generalisations, the latter a better understanding of situations and their likely consequences. *Educational* research is carried out with the explicit intention of improving educational practice or policy by those engaged in the practice.

Elliott's view is that the most congenial research form for this kind of research is the interpretative or practical action research case study, which portrays and explains participants' meanings, actions and intentions, with a view to bringing about research-informed change. As Elliott later argued, it is also educational in the sense that it aims to realise participants' 'educational values in action' (Elliott 2006: 167). This type of research is therefore seen not only as a research approach but also as an invitation to reflect on the ideas and values informing what one does as an educator, and to learn from engaging in research.

We argue later in the chapter that the boundaries between education and educational research are not as impermeable as Elliott's 1978 account implies (Elliott 2006), but for now we acknowledge that the distinction usefully highlights quite radical differences between the two types of research endeavour in education, in terms of purposes, the kind of knowledge aimed at, and the relationship between the researcher and the researched. We examine the main differences in greater detail below, and consider some objections to Elliott's account and to the idea of practitioner research more generally.

Purposes: educational research

Differences in purposes can be brought out by considering some of the questions typical of educational research and education research. The former are usually addressed to practical 'how to' questions raised by individual educators about their practice, or they focus on practical problems that have arisen in the development of common practices across sites. For example, 'How may I improve my teaching of writing history essays?' was the starting point for a secondary school history teacher of 'A' level, who went on to research this problem with his students as co-inquirers (Harris and Foreman-Peck 2001). Similarly, the questions 'How can we improve our understanding of the assessment of prior learning (APL) and the principles informing its award?' are practical questions asked by several academics, responsible for this area of work, collaborating together in two universities (Melrose and Reid 2000).

The examples above illustrate the point that the starting place for educational research is usually a felt dissatisfaction with a current state of affairs in which one is involved and in a certain measure responsible for. This contrasts with education research where there is a wish to contribute to a disciplinary body of knowledge about education or educational topics, but where the connection with teaching is less direct. Examples of such education problems could be fundamental ones that are taken for granted in educational practices in higher education at the moment, or they may address gaps in our knowledge. For instance it is assumed but is by no means certain that so called generic skills, such as problem solving and team work, do transfer to other contexts, such as the workplace.

The primary objective of educational research is to solve or become better informed about a practical problem, so that action can be taken. This requires reflection on what would count as an improvement and, as Swann has argued, a view about what should be preserved in current practice (Swann 2000). This necessitates reflection on the aims of any possible intervention, since effective practice is judged by what we consider to be valuable. An implication of this is that educational researchers need to be aware of their own values and pre-suppositions. Educational research is therefore inevitably concerned with ethical or normative concepts, with what ought to be the case, in a way that other sorts of research do not foreground. It is important to emphasise this at this point, since it is easy to slip into the mistake of supposing that practitioner research is merely concerned with efficiency. For example, getting better results in teaching history writing may be a desirable outcome, but any intervention has to be morally and educationally defensible. Similarly any new method of assessing and awarding APL has to meet certain requirements, for consistency and fairness.

Purposes: education research

Education research, on the other hand, usually has no immediate or explicit practice or policy improvement intention and is usually carried out by professional researchers rather than practitioners, who will not necessarily be engaged in, or even profess an interest in the pedagogical implications of their research. In Elliott's words such researchers are in the position of 'impartial spectators' who 'transcend the evaluative perspectives of education practitioners' (2006: 170).

Such research may inform policy decisions, but this is not necessarily the primary motivation for the research. The motivation is more likely to relate to building the knowledge base of a discipline, as we have said, where the interesting questions are given by the discipline itself. For example the ethnographic work of Brice Heath (1983) which described different approaches to teaching language to infants in two culturally distinct towns in the USA, does not explicitly point to any policy implications. However, it is research that any educator, or policy maker, interested in children's linguistic and emotional development is likely to find interesting and informative, because it seems to explain certain observations and it may suggest possible interventions to improve the lot of certain children. Similarly historical, philosophical, psychological, or social scientific research that takes an aspect of education as its topic, may provide illumination or insight without a direct connection to policy prescriptions or action.

In summary, it is argued by Elliott and others that *educational research* is distinctively practical in orientation, reflective and reflexive, and bound by ethical norms. These characteristics of practitioner research have implications for the kind of knowledge that can be produced, the way in which it is carried out and the way it may appear in the public domain.

Knowledge

Since dissatisfaction with practice arises in the course of one's everyday work, such research starts from and draws on common sense concepts rather than scientific ones. An implication of this position is that *educational research*, as we have already noted, is not scientific, in that it does not use operational or theoretical definitions. This leads some people to assume, mistakenly, that it is not research at all, in the sense that it does not meet standards of scientific rigour, either in its purposes or its methods. In Elliott's (1978) account, the knowledge that educational research produces is the improvement of common sense conceptualisations of practice through critical discourse (1978: 95–96).

Elliott later argued that:

1   Educational research involves 'the development of educational insights and judgements with regard to everyday situations in classrooms and schools' (2006: 171).
2   Educational research involves the Aristotelian idea of phronesis: a 'matter of the formation of good practical ethical judgements' (2006: 171). Elliott interprets

'phronesis' as a distinctive form of practical reasoning that is focused on the rea-lisation of worthwhile educational processes, such as 'autonomous or inde-pendent learning'. The contrast is with technical rationality, where outcomes are tightly pre-specified and the means are regarded as value-neutral.

3 Educational research involves common sense theorising, that is 'a process of continuously constructing and reconstructing the meaning of our value con-cepts in practice' (2006: 173). Educational theories are produced in the context of practice by judgements and actions of teachers. This contrasts with accounts of theory given by the social sciences as explanations that aim to override common sense explanations.

For many people, 'common sense theorising' lacks the authority of social scien-tific knowledge. One reason is because common sense beliefs are often held uncritically. However, as Elliott makes clear, educational research explicitly sets out to question common sense beliefs, and is characterised by a critical stance towards problematic situations. As with other forms of research, a questioning of accepted ideas, based on systematic research and valid reasoning, is crucial. However, the critic of educational research may regard it as less authoritative because, even if it is questioned, it still employs or remains at the level of common sense theo-rising. There are two responses to this implied devaluation of common sense theorising.

First, Pring (2000) argues that, although the contents of many of our common sense beliefs change over time, many are fundamental and indispensible in that they provide the basic framework of our thinking. These ideas cannot be super-seded or overridden by social scientific explanations, for example that there are persons who have intentions and are not reducible to physical objects, and the concepts of time, space, cause and effect (Pring 2000).

Pring argues that theoretical discourse, if it is to be useful, still has to relate to everyday discourse, since the problem addressed is first picked out in everyday discourse and the situation to which it is applied has to be identified in everyday discourse, and related to our basic common sense beliefs (Pring 2000: 86). The rules of practices and the intentions of actors that comprise our common sense are logically prior: theory is only for particular purposes, to explain for instance a particular sort of family relationship or a particular instance of social interaction. For example, the sociologist Goffman introduced the ideas of 'backstage' and 'frontstage', terms derived from the theatre, to depict roles played in everyday social interaction (Goffman 1959).

Second, common sense thinking may be challenged in a number of ways, not only through critical debate, education or disciplinary research but also, as will become apparent in the later sections of this chapter, through practitioner or educational research.

It should be clear by now that educational and *education* research give differ-ent sorts of knowledge. Educational research may provide insights into a localised situation and may issue in practical prescriptions or principles for action. It may also reframe our understanding of problems. It is knowledge that is practically relevant to the teachers who have researched the problem. Education research, on the other hand will aim at knowledge defined by the standards and methods used in the disciplines, such as sociology or ethnography, in which it is embedded.

Relationships

One important consequence of the distinction between educational and education research is, as is probably apparent by now, that the relationship between the researcher and the researched is different. Educational research requires, as a matter of good sense, generally speaking, that students, or others who are party to a problem in practice, become active collaborators in defining the problem, and in some cases, partners in researching it. Indeed, educational action researchers invariably see collaboration as a defining characteristic (see for example Somekh 2006), although the forms of partnership work may take different shapes in different studies. The necessity for collaboration raises ethical and practical issues which differ from those involved in 'research on education', where students or others may figure as 'objects', with no say in the direction of the research. The ethical issues involved in educational research are discussed further in Chapter 9.

Summary

So far we, following Elliott, have argued that:

- *Education research* is research on education carried out by professional or academic researchers, using a range of methodologies from other disciplines, for example economics or ethnography, and is not *primarily* intended to enhance educational practitioners' judgements in localised contexts.
- *Educational research* is research directed at the improvement of educational judgements and practices, carried out by practitioners into their own practices.

Challenges to the distinction between education and educational research

In this section we consider some limitations to the distinction that we have been expounding, since it seems to imply a limited use or relevance to the practice of education research or research on education. We do not wish to argue this. Furthermore it may be objected that the boundaries between education and educational research are not as cut and dried as some versions of the account, offered by Elliott and others, imply.

We consider three objections. First, some education research may be carried out both with the intention of building a body of knowledge *and* improving practice. For example the work of Singley and Anderson (1989) into the transfer of cognitive skill is of interest to educators as well as psychologists, since it addresses fundamental questions about the way in which learning in one context may be generalised by the learner to another context. The complaint that teachers cannot connect such theories with their 'ordinary common sense experience' may be less to do with the perceived irrelevance of the research and more to do with the fact that unless one has a degree in psychology, the research is very difficult for the non-specialist to comprehend. However not all research on education requires a relevant disciplinary training. Some is easily readable and in higher education, for instance, Marton and Saljos' research on deep and surface learners (1984) has been influential in the thinking of higher education practitioners.

Second, some researchers on education may also wish to realise their educational values in practice, through investigating problems that they see as relevant to thorny and endemic issues, such as bullying or disaffection. They may investigate these issues through their disciplinary research even though they may not be directly involved in everyday classroom practice where these problems are sited. To take another example, the question of optimal school size is one that affects the well-being of teachers, parents and children. We know anecdotally from teachers and pupils that schools of over a certain size are difficult to manage well. Large secondary schools are usually justified in economic terms, which ignore possible longer term social and educational costs. Investigating these latter could be of importance to educational policy makers, parents and children (Foreman-Peck and Foreman-Peck 2006).

Third, it could be argued that unless educational research utilises education research where appropriate, it is likely to be uninformed and thus not able to fulfil its promise of building an educator's professional and pedagogic judgements in a credible way. Common sense concepts may be at the core of our understanding of the social world, but they often fail to illuminate problematic situations, or they may suggest simplistic stereotypical responses that are unhelpful. A good example is the case of Gypsy traveller children and the problem of their lack of progress after the primary school phase. Careful ethnographic research can reveal a more complex set of circumstances preventing them from taking part in secondary and further or higher education than is available through folklore, and may suggest new ways of conceptualising their situation (Derrington 2008). Theories derived from research on education or about education can help us to reframe problems, or provide insight or possible hypotheses. Theories which enable teachers to 'discern the practically relevant features of the complex situations they have to handle on a day to day basis' are potentially useful (Elliott 2006: 175). On the other hand, it has to be noted that there are many problematic situations where there is no useful body of education literature to call upon, and teachers may have to generate and test their own theories.

Although the distinction between education and educational research is not watertight, it is not useless. It reminds us that researchers are positioned in different ways to educational practices and have different motivations. The practitioner researcher is not a detached 'spectator' but an engaged part of the educational problem or situation she is researching. The research will have direct consequences for her own thinking about education and for her students' learning, in a way that education research need not. The next section introduces some common practitioner research models and examples which illustrate this point. The models and examples are discussed in more detail in later chapters.

Some common models of educational research

Evaluative case study

The key question underpinning all evaluative educational research is whether a practice, method, intervention, or set of materials works better than alternatives. Thus the current state of affairs has to be evaluated but this evaluative step may be in depth, because it is not clear what the characteristics of an unsatisfactory situation or practice are, or relatively cursory because the nature of the problem has become clear, possibly over a number of years. Evaluations can be carried out at the beginning, and/or during the course of an innovation in order to provide feedback and guidance, and/or they may be carried out at the end of an innovation as a summative judgement on the success or otherwise of the innovation. An example of an evaluative practitioner researcher report by Hartsell and Parker (2008) is given in Chapter 10. Hartsell is the curriculum designer and lecturer, Parker, a student on the course. They evaluated the success of a problem-based approach to teaching social work administration, which was innovative, in that the students worked with real homeless clients. This research was clearly educational for Hartsell and the students in Elliott's terms.

Descriptive case study

A case study is usually defined as a research approach focusing on a single case, or a bounded instance. The case can consist of an individual, a class, an organisation or a situation. Case studies are researched in their contexts. Qualitative data is always collected but quantitative data may also be used. The intention of this kind of case study is in-depth understanding of a situation which is problematic. It may be used to explore actors' perceptions, antecedent conditions, and other factors contributing to a situation. It may focus on describing patterns of interaction between teachers and students, or some aspect of an organisation such as its culture.

Case studies, generally speaking, need not contain an explicit evaluation nor recommendations for practice. However, in educational case study research an element of evaluation and implications for practice would be an expected outcome. For example, a case study carried out by one of the author's M.Ed. students, who was a primary school teacher, focused on the behaviour of one pupil, which showed a contradiction between what she was able to produce in class and her performance in formal tests. The study involved documenting instances of her puzzling behaviour, observing the way in which other pupils related to her, and interviews with other members of staff. The evidence indicated collusion amongst the pupils in hiding from her the fact that the pupil's work was being done by others in the class. Although the emphasis was on understanding the pupil's puzzling behaviour and does not in itself suggest a practical strategy, any action the teacher decided to take would now be informed by a better understanding of what was occurring. This research was educational for the teacher in Elliott's sense.

An example from higher education of a case study utilising a grounded theory approach to data analysis and theory generation, is given in Chapter 10. Howell (2009) interviewed and observed nine occupational therapy students engaged in collaborative learning activities with other health professionals. She wished to understand the way in which occupational therapy students experienced interprofessional education. She found that occupational therapists have a weak sense of professional identity, which disadvantages them in interaction with other professionals. Again, no particular action is suggested by this finding, but any teaching innovation will be informed by it, at least in her own practice.

Action research case study

Action research is also a species of case study in that it focuses on a particular case in a localised context. It differs from the case study approaches described above, in that it usually follows steps, first described by Lewin (1946), and there is an explicit intention to introduce change. These steps are:

- problem specification;
- planning an intervention;
- implementation and monitoring of the intervention;
- evaluation;
- re-specification of the problem (if necessary).

The action research case study may have an element of descriptive case study, as described above, in that the problem may have to be researched before it is clear that it really is a problem, or a problem with the characteristics attributed to it. The research is usually carried out in collaboration with others affected by the problem situation, and they ideally contribute to a plan for an intervention. The intervention is monitored and evaluated either against baseline data or success criteria.

An example of an action research case study in higher education is given in Chapter 10. Parsons and Drew (1996) addressed the problem of student dissatisfaction with group work assessments. They researched the dimensions of the problem, both from their students' and colleagues' points of view and from what had been published in the literature. They hypothesised that at least some of the problem could be addressed by a better designed task and better organisation. They implemented changes along these lines and evaluated the results. The authors were able to evaluate what had been successful and what needed more attention. This research was educational in that the authors tried to align their educational values with their practices in ways that met student dissatisfaction.

It will be apparent that the models presented above have fluid boundaries. Action research, especially the technical version, described in more detail in Chapter 7, may be indistinguishable from an evaluative case study. An evaluation, especially if it takes an illuminative approach (Parlett and Hamilton 1977) may resemble an in-depth case study. The models are, however, useful in that they describe the broad research intentions that practitioner researchers may hold.

We argue that it is helpful for practitioner researchers, and for others who might read their reports, to be clear about their basic research intentions and purposes. In addition, they need to comprehend the relevant extant research literature, where it is available. The education research literature is very diverse, since it covers many disciplines employing different methods and methodologies We have utilised the idea of fixed and flexible designs as a way of sketching out different sorts of research that might be consulted (and in some cases used) by practitioner researchers. These designs are briefly introduced here, and more fully described in Chapter 8.

Types of research: fixed and flexible designs

Robson (2002), drawing on the work of Anastas and MacDonald (1994), makes a useful distinction between fixed and flexible designs. Fixed designs are specifiable in advance and may draw on theory to direct the search for information. Examples are surveys and randomised controlled trials (RCTs). Large scale survey research is usually quantitative and is useful for revealing trends in the population under study. RCTs, which are experiments, are used extensively in medical trials and are useful for suggesting causal connections, for example between drugs and the alleviation of disease. However, the degree of control required by RCTs is not always possible in other settings, and the attempt to use them in educational settings has raised practical and ethical objections which are discussed in Chapters 8 and 9.

Teaching and educational research takes place in 'real' situations, which are complex and unpredictable. In a laboratory, what is done to people can be planned in advance and the experiment very carefully standardised. Some examples of this approach are given in Chapter 9. This is not possible in real educational settings (but see Chapter 8 for a discussion of quasi-experimental research).

Given these difficulties, there has been an interest in flexible designs for research carried out in natural settings. These are not fully specifiable in advance, since they develop as the researcher interacts with other participants in the research. The advantage of this approach is that it allows the researcher to follow up unexpected but possibly more fruitful lines of inquiry. Flexible designs may, however, be seen from some disciplinary perspectives that utilise 'fixed' designs as 'unscientific', in the sense of unsystematic and unprincipled. We will return to this issue in Chapter 8.

Quality issues

Given that educational research is carried out by practitioners whose primary responsibility is teaching and not research and, coupled with the consideration that many will not have received extensive research training, questions have been raised about the quality of such research. In particular, there may be problems in the collection of data, its analysis and its interpretation. If teachers are basing innovations on data or evidence that is questionable, then the action that follows from it, so the argument goes, may not be based on solid grounds.

Much educational research does not find its way into the public domain in terms of publications. Many practitioners do not intend to contribute to a body of knowledge because their primary concern is with solving a practical problem. That said, there are examples where teachers and others have been persuaded to publish, or have been required to publish, as a condition of funding. In reviewing action research reports it became apparent, to one of us, that most practitioners do not have the resources to meet all the quality criteria that are recommended by professional research associations such as the British Educational Research Association (2000) (Foreman-Peck and Murray 2008). Many reports are not fully substantiated. The most obvious omission is the lack of reference to previous research findings. Many published reports took the form of what we termed 'learning accounts'. They described what the teachers did, what happened and whether the intervention appeared to work. Researchers who generated more elaborate accounts published the data their findings were based upon, and their work involved an analysis of the situation before the intervention.

A question that is raised for other practitioners is: 'What sort of credence can these accounts be given?' It is usual to require of research that it is systematic. This is because we wish to be assured that the claims being made are based on more than impressions, unsupported opinions, or indeed blind 'common sense'. Impressionistic claims can be mistaken, anecdotal evidence can be biased, and common sense can be misleading.

It is therefore necessary to be systematic in the collection of data and its analysis, in such a way that another person can follow, critique or test the claims being made. Learning accounts that do not appear to be systematic, or to explicitly discuss the nature of the data or evidence collected and how it was analysed, do not enable the reader to make judgements about the extent to which any claim is trustworthy. On the other hand, some 'learning accounts' which are weak in this respect may nevertheless gain credence because they chime with others' experiences and offer a new way of tackling or understanding a problem.

References to the literature on a topic are also expected as a feature of good research. This is because some findings are already established and it would be a waste of time duplicating them. This is not because they have uncovered truths that hold for all time, but because they allow us to justifiably anticipate a future state of affairs, in relevant contexts. Research, as we saw in Chapter 1, is about making an original contribution to knowledge. In order to make a contribution one needs to know to what one is adding. Of course not all areas in education are well researched. However, some topics, such as assessment, have been extensively researched. Learning accounts that do not make reference to the literature where it exists are in danger of saying nothing interesting to well informed readers. However, they may be of very great interest in areas that are under-researched, or where new problems of practice are emerging.

Teachers and lecturers undertaking educational research for an award will most certainly be required to produce more than 'learning accounts'. They will be required to include literature reviews and to address methodological issues such as validity. Below we list some suggested quality criteria for practitioner research. Some may, of course be applicable to disciplinary research, bur our main concern here is to try to describe the criteria that a good piece of practitioner research would meet.

Quality criteria

- Is the research problem a serious one which is of interest to others in your position (and society in general)?
- Is there an extant body of related research literature that should be consulted?
- Are there any theories that can be usefully drawn upon?
- Have you informed all relevant participants of your intentions and negotiated forms of collaboration?
- Have you observed ethical protocols?
- Is the model of practitioner research you are using clear?
- Are the methods you are using to research this question appropriate to the question(s)?
- Is the collection of data, its analysis and its presentation as transparent as possible?
- Have you interrogated your data/evidence for alternative explanations, in so far as you can?
- Are the conclusions you have drawn from the evidence available to you warranted by the data/evidence?
- Have you formed a reasonable judgement about the degree of confidence others can put in any recommendations or findings you may present?

Exercises

1   Thinking of your own practice as a lecturer or tutor in higher education, what aspects of your teaching would you like to keep and what would you like to change or improve?
2   What do you see as the most urgent issues in higher education? Which are suitable for practitioner research and which for education research? Describe two or three.
3   How do the quality criteria for practitioner research given above differ (if at all) from the quality criteria that apply in your own discipline or field of study?

References

Anastas, J. W. and MacDonald, M. (1994) *Research Design for Social Work and the Human Services*. New York: Lexington Books.

Brice Heath, S. (1983) *Ways with Words: Language, Life and Work in Communities and Classrooms*. Cambridge: Cambridge University Press.

British Educational Research Association (BERA) (2000) *Good Practice in Educational Research Writing*. Available at www.bera.ac.uk/publications/pdfs/goodpr1.pdf (accessed 5.3.08).

Derrington, C. (2008) 'Social Exclusion and Cultural Dissonance as Salient Risk Factors in the Engagement and Retention of Gypsy Traveller Students in Secondary Education'. Unpublished Ph.D. thesis, University of Northampton.

Elliott, J. (1978) 'Classroom Research: Science or Common Sense?' in R. McAleese and D. Hamilton (eds) *Understanding Classroom Life* (pp. 12–15). York: NFER.

——(2006) 'Educational Research as a Form of Democratic Responsibility'. *Journal of the Philosophy of Education, Special Issue: Philosophy, Methodology and Educational Research Part 1* 40, 2: 169–87.

Elliott, J. and Lukes, D. (2008) 'Epistemology as Ethics in Research and Policy'. *Journal of the Philosophy of Education* 42, supplement 1: 87–119.

Foreman-Peck, J. and Foreman-Peck, L. (2006) 'Should Schools Be Smaller? The Size-performance Relationship for Welsh Schools'. *Economics of Education Review* 25: 157–71.

Foreman-Peck, L. and Murray, J. (2008) 'Action Research and Policy'. *Journal of the Philosophy of Education* 42, supplement 1: 145–63.

Glaser, B. G. and Strauss, A. L. (1967) *The Discovery of Grounded Theory: Strategies for Qualitative Research* (pp. 1–35). Chicago: Aldine.

Goffman, E. (1959) *The Presentation of Self in Everyday Life*. New York: Doubleday Anchor.

Harris, R. and Foreman-Peck, L. (2001) 'Learning to Teach History Writing: Discovering What Works'. *Educational Action Research Journal* 9, 1: 97–109.

Hartsell, B. D. and Parker, A. J. (2008) 'Evaluation of Problem-Based Learning as a Method for Teaching Social Work Administration: A Content Analysis'. *Administration in Social Work* 32, 3: 44–62.

Howell, D. (2009) 'Occupational Therapy Students in the Process of Interprofessional Collaborative Learning: A Grounded Theory Study'. *Journal of Interprofessional Care* 23, 1: 667–80.

Lewin, K. (1946) 'Action Research and Minority Problems'. *Journal of Social Issues* 2, 4: 34–46.

Marton, F. and Saljo, R. (1984) 'Approaches to Learning', in F. Marton, D. J. Hounsell. and N. J. Entwistle (eds) *The Experience of Learning*. Edinburgh: Scottish Academic Press.

Melrose, M. and Reid, M. (2000) 'The Daisy Model for Collaborative Action research: Application to Educational Practice'. *Educational Action Research* 8, 1: 151–65.

Parlett, M. and Hamilton, D. (1977) 'Evaluation as Illumination', in M. Parlett and G. Dearden (eds) *Introduction to Illuminative Evaluation*. Studies in Higher Education. Cardiff-by-the-Sea, CA: Pacific Soundings Press.

Parsons, D. E. and Drew, S. K. (1996) 'Designing Group Project Work to Enhance Learning: Key Elements'. *Teaching in Higher Education* 1, 1: 65–80.

Pring, R. (2000) *Philosophy of Educational Research*. London and New York: Continuum.

Robson, C. (2002) *Real World Research: A Resource for Social Scientists and Practitioner-Researchers*. Oxford: Blackwell.

Singley, M. K. and Anderson, J. R. (1989) *The Transfer of Cognitive Skill*. London: Harvard University Press.

Somekh, B. (2006) *Action Research: A Methodology for Change and Development*. Buckingham: Open University Press.

Stenhouse, L. (1980) 'The Study of Samples and the Study of Cases'. *British Educational Research Journal* 61, 1: 1–6.

Swann, J. (2000) 'How Can Research Lead to Improvement in Education?' *Prospero* 6, 3/4: 130–38.

Chapter 4

'Good practice' and evidence-based teaching

What does the claim that evidence supports practice mean?

In Chapter 2, we argued that evidence should support teaching practice in higher education where such evidence is available. But what does the claim that 'evidence should support practice' actually *mean*? Here are four words which both individually and as a sentence are highly ambiguous. So let's unpick this sentence.

Evidence in this context means the use of empirical propositions to provide arguments as to why such and such an action should be taken or why so and so a judgement is justified. The contents of such propositions are statements of fact which should, we argued in Chapter 2, be based on recognised ways of gathering data and inferring, where necessary, generalisations from that data. However, we do not want to exclude the *experiential* evidence of lecturers that arises from prolonged engagement with students in their own subjects and in the contexts of particular universities. Subjectively, such evidence will always carry great weight with individual lecturers and we acknowledge its relevance to the formation of individual judgement. The question for us is not so much whether such evidence is relevant to our actions (it is), but its relationship with evidence gathered in other ways, through, for example, systematic research.

Should signifies a normative requirement, that there is an expectation that evidence will support rather than fail to support practice. It also suggests that, where possible, reasons for action should be based on evidence rather than 'common sense' or 'intuition', although the possibility cannot be excluded that these will have to be relied on in many circumstances.

Support in this context means 'give good grounds for'. There is no one statement of what it is to give good grounds for a proposition. Generally speaking, when the evidence presented is based on generalisation, or on the enumeration of cases, the argument is inductive (Salmon 1984) and should be sound. This means that the evidence should give good, if not conclusive, reasons for acting or for forming a judgement. The possibility is always present, however, that the action may be inappropriate or the judgement mistaken, even when the evidence provides good grounds. But reasons in such a complex area can rarely, if ever, be conclusive. The most that we can strive for is that the reasons given for action or judgement are better supports than any alternative set of reasons that are currently available to us which may suggest a different course of action. If the action or judgement is necessary (e.g. we have to pass comment to a group of students today), then we are obliged to base our actions or judgement on the best considerations that are currently available to us, imperfect though they may be.

Practice refers to the activities of lecturing, discussing, explaining, instructing, demonstrating, arguing, assessing, chairing, etc., that constitute the work of a lecturer engaged in teaching in higher education. We assume, for the purposes of our discussion, that such practices are worthwhile. This means that the ends to which they are directed are worthwhile (they will benefit our students, not to mention the wider society) and that the means which are adopted to achieve those ends are worthwhile as well (they will not violate any ethical requirements of confidentiality or consideration for example). Whether or not our practices are worthwhile in this sense is something that empirical research may have some limited bearing on (e.g. such and such an assessment procedure is not really confidential, despite claims that it is), but is ultimately based on our ideas about what acceptable ways of teaching are. Evidence, therefore, should support practice that we, as a community of lecturers, are prepared to endorse.

Putting all this together, we can argue that 'evidence should support practice' means that it is desirable that, where it is relevant and available, empirical evidence be deployed in order to provide good grounds for actions or judgements that we make in professional contexts, which themselves exist within an ethical framework. This claim can be used to explore the sense in which lecturing is a profession, which we will consider next.

What is a profession? Is lecturing one?

There are no universally agreed criteria for an occupation to qualify as a profession. There are some who consider the morally sensitive nature of a professional's work to be decisive. Others draw attention to the role of knowledge in a professional's activity, others emphasise legal status, and others again suggest that possession of a sufficient bundle of professional traits confers the title 'profession' on an occupation. These traits include those mentioned above together with mechanisms of control of entry and access to the professional labour market. The position is further complicated by the claimed existence of 'semi-professions' (Etzioni 1969) which possess some professional traits but insufficient to characterise them as fully fledged professions. Teaching is often thought to fall into this category.

It would be natural to think that, on the criterion of knowledge possession, a teacher would be a professional. It is, however, sometimes questioned whether the knowledge possessed by a teacher, particularly a primary school teacher, is sufficiently more detailed than that of a reasonably educated member of the public to qualify as specialist knowledge. It is therefore sometimes claimed that it is the knowledge of how children learn and develop that constitutes the core of a teacher's claim to professional knowledge. It is obvious that university lecturers possess far more knowledge in their areas of expertise than do educated members of the public. In this sense, the claim to specialist knowledge on the part of lecturers is relatively secure. This consideration also secures their status as professionals, since the knowledge that they possess is, in most cases, abstract, extensive and difficult to acquire, just like the knowledge possessed by other professions such as the law and medicine. Indeed, it is quite reasonable to claim that the achievement of a Ph.D. is not only a demonstration of the acquisition of specialist knowledge and skill, but is itself built upon an extensive background knowledge of a subject.

On the other hand, as described above, lecturers' professional knowledge differs in one important respect to that of doctors and lawyers. Both doctors and lawyers are expected to *apply* their specialist knowledge in operational situations, rather than *expound* it (although this may be a secondary role). The core of their claim to professional expertise thus lies in their ability to use esoteric knowledge in complex operational situations to generate professional judgements and courses of action (Eraut 1994). Lecturers are expected to *generate* new subject knowledge and to *expound* existing knowledge. The former role requires the skill of a researcher which may or may not be classed as professional knowledge. If it is, it will be so for the same reason as the doctor is classified as a professional, namely the *application* of esoteric knowledge in operational situations which requires skill in handling existing knowledge in order to generate new knowledge.

However, the role of lecturer seems to require nothing more than the exposition of existing esoteric knowledge. One's professionalism as a *lecturer* rather than as an academic in a broader sense seems to rest on this ability. It is far from clear that this requires a special skill. If this is so, then lecturer professionalism seems to rest on possession of specialist academic knowledge rather than on ability to apply that knowledge. Attempts to align the teacher's claim to professionalism through possession of a specialist body of knowledge of how children learn and develop, which they then deploy in professional judgement, seems to founder on the fact that, even were we to acknowledge that teachers do indeed possess such knowledge (see Chapter 2), it is not relevant to lecturers, who teach adults, not children. One may ask, is there any specialist knowledge that one needs concerning how adults learn in order to teach them? If the answer is 'no', then the claim that lecturers need to acquire such knowledge in order to develop the skill of teaching is weakened. If the teaching of adults is a practical skill, then supervised practice overseen by a seasoned and experienced lecturer ought to suffice. Lecturing would be a skill, but not one that required systematic propositional knowledge in order to practice it. Lecturers would largely gain their position as professionals through their abilities as researchers rather than as teachers.

If this were to be the case, then a professional qualification for lecturing would be largely centred around the acquisition of skill in conducting lectures, handling seminars, giving tutorials and marking assignments and field and lab work, which could all, arguably, be done through supervised practice. This is admittedly a plausible proposition which must be taken seriously. In what follows we will examine it.

Schön's ideas: unclarity on reflection in and on action

One of the most influential accounts of the cognitive aspects of professionalism is the work of Donald Schön (1991), who developed the ideal of the professional as a *reflective practitioner*. Schön's account, originally developed with architects in mind, has been particularly influential in nursing and teaching. It is centred around the claim that professional activity is fluid, complex and unpredictable and that successful practitioners navigate their working lives, not through the conscious application of theory to practice, but through a process of ongoing thinking about their activity. The model of professionalism that Schön is particularly opposed to is what he calls *technical rationality*, or the claim that professional activity depends on the more or less conscious application of scientific, theoretical or abstract knowledge to professional problems.

Since the employment of technical rationality in this sense is just what, it was argued in Chapter 2, constituted the mark of a professional worker, Schön's claim seems to undermine that approach and to suggest a different one. We need, therefore, to examine the claim that technical rationality is an inadequate account of professional action and to enquire whether reflection provides a persuasive alternative characterisation.

Schön distinguishes between two kinds of reflection: *reflection in action* and *reflection on action*. It is clear that he thinks that the former is of more importance in professional activity than the latter. Central to his thinking is the claim (undoubtedly a true one in most cases) that a professional has to work in complex operational conditions in which decisions are required very quickly, mistakes are not easily rectified and where new and unexpected situations constantly occur which require rapid judgement and decision taking. In such situations a professional has to exercise judgement by bringing previous experience to bear on a problem in the field. Since experience, by its nature, can only be acquired over time, the ability to reflect is one that can only be fully acquired by a mature professional. Schön's central claim is, then, that professional workers make operational judgements very quickly on the basis of accumulated experience and that this judgement occurs as a result of reflection during the time frame within which the need for a decision presents itself and has to be reached. Furthermore, the reflection has to be on previous personal professional experience, as Schön maintains that reflection on the relevance of theory to practice is largely irrelevant to successful decision making. In this respect, his position has strong affinities to Oakeshott's conception of practical knowledge, outlined in Chapter 2.

There is little doubt much professional decision making does take place in such circumstances in which the action is 'hot' (i.e. decisions are time-critical and there is no opportunity for withdrawal for reflection: Beckett and Hager 2002). But it may be doubted whether anything worthy of the name of reflection could be attempted in such circumstances. Reflection, by its nature, requires a 'cool' place in which to occur and 'hot' environments, while they may require judgement, are not conducive to reflection. Schön appears to be confusing *reflection* with *judgement*.

In order to reflect one needs a certain physical and psychological distance from action. This is not necessarily the case with judgement.

Judgement, like reflection, is episodic or at least semi-episodic (Geach 1958). One may soliloquise and then act or one may just act. Depending on the circumstances we might describe both cases and a variety of others in between as instances of professional judgement. One can allow that in some instances of 'hot action' someone may be able to go through a process of more or less conscious reasoning before acting, even if such a process does not really merit the title 'reflection'. There is no reason to suppose, however, that such processes of 'thinking on one's feet' depend solely on one's previous professional experience rather than on the theoretical knowledge that underpins the professional activity. If it only relied on the former it would be difficult to see what the point of underpinning theoretical knowledge was in relation to professional judgement.

Schön is on much stronger ground when he talks about reflection *on* action. This takes place beyond the confines of 'hot' professional environments, where there is time for recollection and consideration, which seems to be a necessary rather than contingent condition for the availability of reflection. Here again, there is no reason to believe that professional reflection should not be based on underpinning theory, as well as previous professional experience. Indeed, one would expect such reflection to include features such as the use of theoretical and research background to try and diagnose the nature of problems that have arisen in unexpected situations, together with consideration of similarities and differences with previously encountered situations. It is a mistake to counterpose theory/research with experience as mutually exclusive candidate components of professional judgement. The difficulty is in showing how they combine. This is something that we attempted to give an account of in Chapters 2 and 6.

The ethical conception of professionalism

One influential strand of thinking about the nature of professional education is that its distinctive characteristic is *ethical*, which is to say that it is primarily concerned with the quality of commitment to the human objects of professional concern: students, patients, clients, parishioners (Carr 2000). It is sometimes claimed that other occupations do not share the same intensity of ethical commitment or even that it is possible to be a good practitioner while behaving in an ethically unacceptable way, whereas this is not possible for a professional (e.g. Carr 2000). This way of putting the matter seems to make intrinsic ethical concern a defining characteristic of professions and hence of professional activity. It is a view that contrasts quite strongly with the views of professionalism that we have so far looked at, but which has, nevertheless, affinities with them.

Whether or not this account of what it is to be a professional is correct is something that we will address below. At this point, however, we would like to point out that it would still need to be established whether lecturing was a profession in this sense, even if we were to accept the ethical account of professionalism.

In order to understand the claim, it is helpful to return to the concept of *practical knowledge* looked at before in Chapter 2. Practical knowledge in Oakeshott's sense involves engagement with others in a common enterprise. One could say then that ethical engagement is *intrinsic* to the possession of practical knowledge. This does not, of course, mean that one can be instructed in practical knowledge – rather it develops through an extended process of involvement in a practice. The personal attributes that one needs in order to work with or interact with other people, such as consideration, patience, generosity, sympathy, are developed through engagement, through reflection and example. Such attributes, traditionally termed 'virtues', are aspects of character and are manifested in one's everyday professional and social activity and form the basis on which others form attitudes to oneself, in terms of whether one is trustworthy, reliable, a good colleague and so on.

One aspect of professional virtue is worth noting. Some virtues are necessary to carry out the detailed specifications of one's work successfully. The 'narrow' virtues of scholarship are necessary for an academic: curiosity, patience, thoroughness and attention to detail. Other-regarding virtues such as a love of truth, humility, generosity and open-mindedness are also important. All of these apply to teaching as much as to research and scholarship. But beyond these are arguably such virtues as courage and civic engagement, which reflect awareness of the broader aspects of one's work as a teacher and academic which concern the implications of what one does within the broader society in which one lives (Kerschensteiner 1964). It goes without saying that the other virtues mentioned also play a role in this wider civic engagement. Love of truth is not just a private matter in one's research but affects the way in which results are presented to a broader public as well.

Critique of ethical professionalism

The ethical account of professionalism is inadequate. But this is not because ethics is unimportant for professional activities – it most certainly is important. However, there are two important respects in which it needs modifying.

The first is that ethics is not peculiar to professions as opposed to other occupations (for a contrasting view, see Carr 1999). Just as one can be a good technical butcher or carpenter but a bad one ethically in the sense that one treats one's customers badly or that one pays little attention to, for example, the environmental impact of one's activities, so one can be a good lawyer or lecturer in the technical sense but a bad one ethically in just the same way. A technically good carpenter will know how to design, build and evaluate artefacts but may, for example, be inclined to cheat customers and suppliers. A little reflection will show that exactly the same is true of a lawyer or a lecturer. Technically good but ethically lacking lawyers and carpenters fail to be good carpenters or lecturers in exactly the same senses – they miss out on some of the most important virtues that make their occupations honourable ones.

But the conception of the ethics of an occupation that only focuses on relationships with customers, suppliers, colleagues, apprentices and regulators is inadequate in another sense. Any occupation has ramifications beyond the effects that it has on those most immediately concerned with the occupational activities. The broader public are affected as well. A lecturer who fails to prepare lectures and seminars or to assess work properly not only affects his students and his university but, indirectly, the broad public who pay for and benefit from good historians, teachers, lawyers, businessmen, etc. There is, in other words, a *civic* dimension to professional ethical responsibility as well as a personal one.

But the ethical conception of professionalism is also inadequate because it is an incomplete description of the *non-ethical* aspects of professional activity. It is fundamental to nursing that nurses have the kind of care and concern for their patients that contribute to the patients' well-being, but if they are unable to bedwash, feed, take temperatures or administer medicines competently, they will never be good nurses. And in fact, once one has put the point like this, one also comes to understand the futility of relying solely on either ethical or technical categories in order to understand professionalism. It is part of good technical nursing or lecturing that one has a concern, not just for getting it right, but for excellence in what one does. One could not be an ethically concerned professional without at least trying very hard to be good at the technical aspect of what one does. To describe professionalism as ethical practice without drawing attention to the technical aspect of one's job is just to misunderstand one important part of what it is to be ethically concerned about one's work.

But occupational and professional ethics are also concerned with the implications of one's work beyond the confines of the workplace, about its impact on the public. It is possible to fully exemplify the 'bourgeois virtues' (to use Kerschensteiner's expression) of individual occupational excellence, without an understanding of the 'civic virtues' of wider occupational responsibility (Kerschensteiner, 1964). Commentators like Carr are right to be concerned with the vital nature of attention to such matters in the work of professionals. But the need is just as acute for non-professionals. Both professionals and non-professionals can be technically excellent or even virtuous while showing a lack of civic responsibility. But this shows that civic virtue is, although a necessary feature of a fully-developed professional excellence, not something that differentiates professions from other occupations. We can conclude, therefore, that there is nothing ethically distinctive about the professions as opposed to other occupations.

Towards a conception of professionalism in teaching and lecturing

It is now possible to examine what is distinctive about professionalism in teaching and lecturing. We have spoken about giving due recognition to the ethical dimension of occupational excellence in a broad sense. It is now time to look more closely at the more technical requirements of professionalism in teaching and lecturing.

We suggested that a key feature of any such professionalism should be a serious engagement with evidence that supports an ethically defensible set of aims for the occupation. We also argued that a significant part of any such evidence should arise from systematic empirical research *where such research is available*. We further argued that in many cases it was not, and that it was desirable that it should be made available. It cannot be the *primary* responsibility of those engaged in an occupation to be responsible for research into the conduct of that occupation, at least in those cases where pursuit of and research into the occupation are distinct activities, as they are in most cases. The occupation of academic appears to present an interesting counter-example to this claim, however, as it appears to involve both research and teaching. Admittedly, the object of the research of an academic will normally be an aspect of the subject matter which he or she teaches, and, unless that academic is a specialist in pedagogy in higher education, it is likely that the subject of his or her research will be distinct from the nature of the teaching that is carried out.

This suggests that lecturers in higher education do not have a primary responsibility to carry out research into effective pedagogy in their own subject at the higher education level, even though they normally do have such a responsibility in the subject matter which they teach. The most that we could expect would be a secondary responsibility, meaning that they need to pay attention to research carried out into higher education pedagogy. In this respect, they would not differ from teachers in other phases of education. But most teachers need a 'licence to practice' which includes a teaching qualification, before they can teach, at least within the state sector of education. To some extent (arguably, not to a sufficient extent) that qualification includes development of the ability to pay intelligent and critical attention to research on teaching and learning. Normally, teachers will not be expected to carry out such research at a professional level during their careers. However, they may well have to carry out a research project as part of their professional qualification. This will at least give them some insight into the demands of research, even if it is not sufficient to enable them to practice research at an original and publishable level. It is plausible to argue though, that without some understanding of the way in which evidence supports judgements about pedagogical practice, they will be, to some extent, bereft of support for professional judgement.

To see why this is so, it may be helpful to look at the notion of 'good practice' in teaching. The term 'good practice' is much used in a variety of professional contexts, both inside and outside lecturing. However, as Alexander (1992) pointed out, it is also systematically ambiguous. Following Alexander's analysis, four distinct uses of the term can be distinguished:

1 Good practice accords with my aims and values.
2 Good practice is the practice that I feel comfortable with.
3 Good practice is what I have the authority to impose on others.
4 Good practice is that practice which the evidence suggests best achieves the aims of the activity.

(adapted from Alexander 1992)

The logical relationships between these stipulative definitions are interesting. Thus definition 3, which means that good practice is what A tells B to do because A is in a position of authority to do so can be supported by 1, 2 or 4 and very often is supported by 1 or 2, rather than 4. Definitions 1 and 2 are both consistent with 4, but 1 and 4 may be incompatible if, for example, *my* aims and values are not those primarily associated with the activity. In such a case, 1 would need *prima facie* to be rejected. Likewise, if 4 fails to support 2, then there is a *prima facie* case for rejecting 2, even if my reasons for supporting 2 amount to an appeal to common sense. However, we saw in Chapter 2, the appeal to common sense is not a strong one when it comes to justification for practices whose application is sensitive to evidential considerations. Evidence may be available for a course contra-indicative to the suggestions of common sense, precisely because appeals to common sense usually have a strongly subjective element to them, whereas appeals to evidence at least aim for objectivity. Now of course it could not be the case that, merely because evidence contra-indicative to common sense or to experience was available, it should imply that it should prevail. That would be to abdicate one's critical faculties and to fail to subject evidence to critical assessment. It is only when evidence conforms to canons of robustness and sound inference that it can be used to prevail over other well-grounded considerations.

It appears then that not only is definition 1 subordinate to 4 in case of conflict, but so is 2 (given the proviso in the previous paragraph). It further follows that even if someone has the *formal* authority (traditional, charismatic or legal-rational in Weber's terminology) to dictate what 'good practice' should amount to, to dictate to others what they should do, they cannot posses the *moral* authority to do so if the reasons that they have rest on 1 or 2 and these are contradicted either evidentially or in value terms by 4. In this sense, the appeal to 4 'trumps' appeals to 1, 2 and 3 and suggests that where good evidence is available to support a course of action in conformity with the agreed values of an occupation, it must be taken seriously. If it is not immediately available, but is obtainable, then attention should be paid to attaining it if at all possible.

If this line of argument is correct then it suggests that a lecturer would be predisposed to paying attention to evidence to support pedagogic practice where such evidence is available. Of course, in many cases such evidence is not available. Indeed, there are many cases where a course of action is recommended to colleagues by 'academic managers' for which no good evidence is available. In such cases, where 'good practice' is identified with definition 3 (e.g. 'all lecturers should use Powerpoint presentations in all their classes – order of the Head of Department') professional probity suggests that such an edict be questioned in the light of what evidence is available to support the use of such a practice as a pedagogic enhancement. In this kind of case, it would seem that common sense would prevail. However, the point of the example is that it is, in such cases, not just legitimate but *desirable* to ask for evidence to support a practice which involves considerable expense and changes to established practices, especially if good reasons or evidence can be offered for existing practice. Not just any evidence would do either in order to persuade a sceptical lecturer that he or she should adopt Powerpoint in every class. The evidence would have to be strong enough to constitute a serious objection to continuing with established practice. And, were it to be adopted, it would still be subject to evaluation by the lecturer who had adopted it. To do otherwise would be to fail to be sensitive to evidential considerations.

Distinctive characteristics of a professional lecturer

There are three main conclusions to the arguments presented in this chapter. The first is that lecturing, like any other occupation, embodies professional aims and values and that these constitute the moral scaffolding of the practice. They are more than an individual ethic, however, but constitute an occupational community defined by the aims of the activity and its responsibilities to those it serves and, indeed, to the broader society (see Carr 1999; Winch 2002 for more on this issue).

The second is that practice should be sensitive to evidential considerations within the moral scaffolding that constitutes the virtues, duties and rights associated with the occupation. Lecturing is an occupation whose practices are very much underdetermined by available evidence, which, in many cases is either not available or is too weak to determine courses of action. But this is not a desirable situation, particularly when innovation is constantly being suggested without sufficiently good reasons being offered for why it should be adopted. We claim that, where possible, evidence should be offered that constitutes grounds that are better than any other available for adopting or not adopting a particular course of pedagogic action.

This consideration leads us to our third conclusion, that lecturers have a responsibility to pay attention to evidence where it is available and to have working knowledge of what are canons of good evidence in *educational* research. This, we think, further entails that, in the early stages of their pedagogic careers, lecturers should at least undertake a small research project into pedagogical issues that are relevant to them in order to gain practical experience of the difficulties and possibilities available in educational research.

Exercises

1   You work in a research-active university in which there is constant pressure to free up time for research. Your head of department has suggested that the department teaches too intensively and that the customary three-hour teaching sessions on your master's programme be reduced to two hours, maintaining that there will be no loss of quality. As a lecturer on this programme, responsible for one of the modules, you are very anxious that the loss of one third of teaching contact time does not adversely affect the quality of student learning. Discuss possible responses to this request utilising the analysis of good practice given in the chapter.

2 To what extent do you agree that a lecturer's professionalism consists of more than subject expertise?
3 What do you see as the place of research-derived evidence in lecturing?

References

Alexander, R. (1992) *Policy and Practice in the Primary School.* London: Routledge.

Beckett, D. and Hager, P. (2002) *Life, Work and Learning.* London: Routledge.

Carr, D. (1999) 'Professional Education and Professional Ethics'. *Journal of Applied Philosophy* 16, 1: 33–46.

——(2000) *Professionalism and Ethics.* London: Routledge.

Eraut, M. (1994) *Developing Professional Knowledge and Competence.* London: Falmer Press.

Etzioni, A. (ed.) (1969) *The Semi-Professions and their Organization: Teachers, Nurses and Social Workers.* London: Collier-Macmillan.

Geach, P. (1958) *Mental Acts.* London: Routledge.

Kerschensteiner, G. (1964) *Ausgewählte Pädagogische Texte.* Vol. 1. Paderborn: Schöningh.

Salmon, W. (1984) *Logic.* Englewood Cliffs, NJ: Prentice-Hall.

Schön, D. (1991) *The Reflective Practitioner: How Professionals Think in Action.* Aldershot: Avebury.

Winch, C. (2002) 'Work, Well-being and Vocational Education'. *Journal of Applied Philosophy* 19, 3: 261–71.

Chapter 5

Handle with care

Reading and evaluating research

The requirements of research in education

In Chapter 3 we introduced the distinction between educational and education research, suggesting that the distinction between practically oriented (educational) and non-practically oriented (education) research, although useful for some purposes, is also arbitrary. John Elliott argues that the education researcher adopts the view of an *impartial spectator*, whereas the educational researcher is engaged and explicit about the values adopted in the research. It is further implied that this distinction also marks a distinction in *genre* between an academic research article or paper on the one hand and a research report on the other. This difference in *genre* in methodological approach is reflected in differences in the way in which the research is reported. Thus education research tends to be reported in refereed academic journals and educational research in professional ones.

Our belief is that this account is oversimplified. In particular, we question the claim that a researcher approaching an issue from the point of view of systematic study (as opposed to subjective interpretation) is, or could be an *impartial observer*, even if he or she wanted to be. Both educational and education researchers have their own values and points of view on educational issues, and these are bound to affect their perceptions of the situation which they propose to study, even if they are doing so from the point of view of systematic, non-subjective investigation. The implied analogy with a natural scientist in a laboratory is misleading, as there are very good reasons for thinking that conceptually speaking, social research in general and educational research in particular are qualitatively different in important respects from research in the natural sciences. However, the fact that a researcher of educational issues cannot be an impartial observer in this sense imposes particular responsibilities. One must therefore access educational research with a view to asking whether these responsibilities are being fulfilled or, better, whether an honest attempt has been made to fulfil them. The contrary of 'impartial' is 'partial', which would imply that a researcher, whether an education or an educational one, will have their own point of view. On the other hand, no-one would want a researcher to be *subjective*, that is to look at matters only from their own point of view. Even a researcher looking at their own practice has to maintain standards of *objectivity*, that is, to describe matters how they are, rather than how they seem. And, if this is impossible, they must clearly state when a subjective stance is being adopted so that the reader can form their own judgement about what is being claimed.

The first thing to look for in either a research article or a research report is a sustainable link between the claims that are being made by authors, for example that such and such processes are taking place in a seminar, or that so and so factors influence examination results, and these claims being underpinned by sufficiently robust evidence and argumentation. At its simplest level this may entail no more than a presentation of the evidence: such and such processes did actually take place in the lectures observed. There is then no need for further argument – the evidence may be sufficient, if, for example, one wished to draw conclusions only about the lectures observed. However, this is unlikely. In most cases, conclusions will be drawn that apply beyond particular observations or cases. In those cases, and they will be nearly all, *argument* will be required to take the researcher from the evidence presented to the conclusion offered. One might argue that the kind of research report that describes a single case is, nevertheless, useful in providing some insight into a question, even if it is not *objective* in the sense that it is subject to criteria of evaluation that all can agree with.

We are happy to concede this, even to the extent that literary examples can provide such illumination. Kingsley Amis's *Lucky Jim* is not a factual account of a provincial English university in the early 1950s, but provides some insight into the cultural milieu of such institutions at that time (limited because arguably based on one or two particular institutions). Likewise, the *Bildungsroman* tradition of novels in the Germanic countries offers insights into the German educational concept of *Bildung* which might be difficult to obtain through other methods. Nevertheless, it is most unlikely that anyone would suggest acting as if the events described in *Lucky Jim* or *Green Henry* (by Gottfried Keller) were true. In cases like these, a subjective account is being openly offered, which the reader is free to take as they wish. Likewise the reports of individual teachers or lecturers of their own work may provide understanding. We are likely to take them as true accounts and thus *objective* (unlike the literary examples above), but will not necessarily believe that they are replicable in our own seminars, tutorials or lectures. For a claim that they are applicable we need an argument that what is reported in the research has wider applicability beyond the arena of the research itself. Note that we are not claiming that the warrant for that wider applicability should constitute *proof* that what is reported is indeed of wider applicability, but rather that it should give us good grounds for supposing that to be the case, or, at the very least, good grounds for supposing that the adoption of a certain approach will, in the right conditions, lead to similar results. These grounds should be available to all who read the report.

How to read educational research

Reports available in professional journals often do not meet this demand. This is not necessarily a fault since they may not aim to produce a warrant for recommending adopting a certain practice or a certain stance, other than the personal experience of the author. It is reasonable to expect refereed academic journals, however, to do just that. This is why, on the whole, we look to such quarters for guidance on what might be sustainable innovative practice. We are entitled to look for arguments and evidence that are susceptible to objective evaluation. This means some degree of *replicability* and the possibility of anyone competent reconstructing and evaluating the argument presented. Thus the 'impartial observer' stance suggested by John Elliott is an oversimplification. Researchers who are committed to their results and to the practical relevance and value of what they are doing need to be able to convince their readers that their assertions are warranted. It should, therefore, be possible, through reading their research reports in a refereed journal, to access the evidence and the arguments that lead from evidence to conclusion and to evaluate the quality of both the evidence and the argument that takes one from the evidence to the conclusion. Where this is not fully possible, there should be what Bassey (1999) calls an 'audit trail', which takes one from the claims to the original evidence on which those claims are based. At a more fundamental level it is also necessary that the claims being made by researchers are intelligible and that they are so in a way that allows empirical evidence for them to be assessed. This is not the case when, for example, central concepts relating to the claim are unclear, or when evaluative and descriptive elements are brought together in a concept without the distinction between them being made clear, as in the case of the distinction between *deep* and *surface learning*, which we discuss below.

What is known about the use of research from empirical studies on higher education teaching?

Research into pedagogical practice in higher education is not in a very advanced state. The problems that have hindered advances in understanding in other areas of education have had a tendency to re-appear in the HE context. Given that we have argued that research in education is still in a relatively undeveloped state and that the field is complex and difficult to research, it is not at all surprising to find these problems in HE pedagogical research as well. As might be expected with a discipline in its infancy, the problems do not just concern the carrying out and interpretation of empirical investigations, but the conceptual presuppositions that underlie such research. As we shall see in the examples below, this is characteristic of much of the research in this area. If the conceptual foundations of an empirical research project are flawed, we cannot expect very much that is useful to emerge from the research that starts from such presuppositions. The problem with the research is sometimes a different one, but is often found in conjunction with the first, namely that evaluative and descriptive elements are found together in the same claim, with the result that what should be a hypothesis turns out to look more like a persuasive definition and hence difficult, if not impossible, to validate or invalidate empirically, thus failing to meet the requirement of *objectivity*. A careful conceptual account of the problem to be researched is not, therefore, an optional extra, but a prerequisite of successful research.

Learning styles

One of the major movements in pedagogical prescription, which has been widely taken up in different sectors of education, including HE, and even received a degree of official endorsement, is the claim that teachers should take account of and work with individual learners' preferred *learning* styles. Thus learner A may prefer to learn primarily through a visual medium, B through an audial one and C through tactile means. Pedagogical strategies should be tailored to these individual preferences. But what evidence is there for such claims? More fundamentally, are they coherent claims? These important questions have not been raised with sufficient force about this line of research.

There is a fundamental review of the literature and research on learning styles by Coffield et al. (2004) which casts serious doubt on the claims made by advocates of teaching according to learning styles. The problem, then, with the research on learning styles evaluated by Coffield et al. is not merely that the warrants fail to support the claims, but more fundamentally that the claim that there are different learning styles has not been coherently formulated. For the claim is not the uncontroversial one that people learn in different ways in different circumstances in relation to different subject matters, but rather that different individuals adopt different characteristic ways of learning *irrespective* of the context or the material to be learned. This claim, in turn, rests on a further assumption about the underlying neurological organisation and orientation of the learner in question. These assumptions are based largely on speculation. And such claims, implicit or explicit, remain just that – assumptions. A little reflection suggests that to hold that there are different learning styles in this stronger sense is an implausible claim. Mastery of an audial medium, like speaking a foreign language for example, can hardly be accomplished through other than audial means; mastery of a manual skill such as wielding a chisel requires appropriate manual dexterity; and so on. This is little more than tautological. However, the claim that one can learn to play a musical instrument purely by visual or tactile means is not far short of nonsensical.

Learning styles research confuses two issues. The first is the relatively uncontroversial claim, first, that different individuals may go about learning particular knowledge, skills, etc., in different ways and, second, that they may prefer those ways in those kinds of situations. Few are likely to dispute such claims. The second issue is the much more controversial set of claims that (a) there are persistent preferences for learning in a particular kind of way *irrespective of the subject matter to be mastered*, and (b) that such preferences are, ultimately, rooted in neurological orientation and organisation. It is primarily in the latter set of claims that research into and claims concerning learning styles are rooted. The literature available in this area suggests that such claims, which come in a number of different forms, have an inadequate empirical base for the purpose of pedagogic prescription (Coffield et al. 2004).

But before we can assess the strength or otherwise of the empirical base for such claims, we need to be clear about whether or not they ultimately make sense. A 'learning style inventory' purports to be valid, that is to provide an accurate measure of some underlying property of the subject to whom the inventory is applied. But whether or not there is such an underlying property is the main question to be answered, and the distribution of scores of a subject on a learning styles inventory cannot, by itself, answer that question. The reliability of any such instrument, although it may protect the learning styles theorist against any immediate dismissal of the validity of the instrument, does not provide evidence of its validity. Indeed, it is hard to see how it could do so, since the claims rest on particular conceptualisations of learning which ultimately have little or nothing to do with empirical research but a great deal to do with philosophical speculation about the nature of learning and, in some cases, about the neurological basis of learning (see Bakhurst 2008 for more on this). Thus the neo-Deweyan speculations of Kolb about feedback loops in learning are sometimes linked to philosophical speculation about the relationship between understanding of a learning task and the way in which the brain and nervous system is 'wired' to facilitate the processing of information through different channels: visual, tactile, audial, etc.

Such speculations usually embody fundamental confusions about the relationship between *understanding*, a concept based on the grasp of normative features of the world, and *neurological processing*, which is a concept in biology based on the search for a *nomological* explanation of the behaviour of cellular and, possibly, subcellular phenomena in the human nervous system. Two distinct *categories* of explanation, the normative and the nomological, are confused (Bennett and Hacker 2003; Hutchinson et al. 2008). It is not, therefore, surprising that the empirical evidence for such speculations is difficult to obtain, given the confused nature of the research question that learning styles theory has formulated. But even a satisfactory empirical confirmation in terms of a stable relationship between, for example, the adoption of subjectively preferred learning styles and scholastic success, should it ever appear, ought to leave us cautious in our interpretation of such results. Results based on flawed conceptual foundations ought to leave us inclined to look for alternative, more coherent explanations for the results that we have achieved (Lipton 2004). Although highly influential, learning styles theories still have some way to go before they receive a satisfactory formulation, let alone robust enough empirical confirmation to serve as a basis for pedagogic prescription.

Deep and surface learning

The second example we shall consider involves grasping, once again, the distinction between deep and surface learning, which is often characterised as a series of contrasts on a nominal scale. A typical example of the contrasts is made in Table 5.1.

Table 5.1 Deep and surface learning

Deep	Surface
Focus is on 'what is signified'.	Focus is on the 'signs' (or on the learning as a signifier of something else).
Relates previous knowledge to new knowledge.	Focus on unrelated parts of the task.
Relates knowledge from different courses.	Information for assessment is simply memorised.
Relates theoretical ideas to everyday experience.	Facts and concepts are associated unreflectively.
Relates and distinguishes evidence and argument.	Principles are not distinguished from examples.
Organises and structures content into a coherent whole.	Task is treated as an external imposition.
Emphasis is internal, from within the student.	Emphasis is external, from demands of assessment.

Source: Based on Ramsden 1988: 47.

The features of deep and surface approaches can also be summarised thus:

Surface

1 Learning as a *quantitative increase in knowledge*. Learning is acquiring information or 'knowing a lot'
2 Learning as *memorising*. Learning is storing information that can be reproduced.
3 Learning as acquiring facts, skills and methods that can be *retained and used* as necessary.

Deep

4 Learning as *making sense* or abstracting meaning. Learning involves relating parts of the subject matter to each other and to the real world.
5 Learning as interpreting and *understanding reality in a different way*. Learning involves comprehending the world by re-interpreting knowledge.

(Saljo 1979)

In this schema, 1–3 are examples of surface learning, 4–5 examples of deep learning.

Although both these examples suggest a descriptive categorisation of two different kinds of learning, closer examination of both classifications suggests that there is a normative element to them. It is being suggested, not only that there are different kinds of learning, but that one kind is better than another. So, for example, if one considers examples of surface learning from Ramsden we find the following descriptions:

> Information for assessment is *simply memorised.*
> Facts and concepts are *associated unreflectively.*
> Task is treated as an *external imposition.*

The italicised phrases highlight pejorative references to features of surface learning. As descriptions, they could read as:

> Information for assessment is *memorised.*
> Facts and concepts are *associated.*
> Task is treated as an *external* requirement.

and their pejorative connotations would be largely removed. The point that we are making about this research is that the way in which it should be read and understood is not straightforwardly like an account of an experiment in one of the natural science disciplines. It is suggested here that some forms of learning are better than others and the ways in which these two contrasting types of learning are categorised is not simply or even at all a matter of empirical investigation into types of learning, but to some extent an a priori categorisation of the kinds of learning that the authors consider desirable. The effect is achieved through *persuasive definition* and the persuasive effect is largely removed through the removal of the pejorative aspects of the description. Note that doing so does not invalidate the possibility of conducting an empirical enquiry into different types of learning that may or may not fall under these descriptors.

It is quite possible, for example, to investigate forms of learning that depend on the memorisation of information, the association of facts and concepts and the requirement that a task should be fulfilled, that depend on the effectiveness of relating new to previously acquired knowledge, on relating evidence to argument and which relate knowledge from different sources. Such forms of learning could then be compared for their relative efficacy according to some understood and agreed criterion of efficacy, which would involve an account of what has been learned and the quality of the learning achieved. However, such an investigation could not be carried out if learning as a *task* has not been clearly distinguished from learning as an *achievement* (cf. Ryle 1949). It is not clear whether such a distinction has been made in the table above, although most of the items appear to treat learning as a task rather than as an achievement, but there is a very good reason to suppose that any measure of the success of deep learning as a process or task should result in a superior level of knowledge and understanding as an achievement to that which would have arisen from a process of surface learning. Such a project could well be valuable, but one cannot assume before an investigation has been carried out that the results of such a study will incline in one way rather than another. The problem with the 'pejorative' descriptors of surface learning is that they establish a quasi-logical link between task and process, such that superficial learning (in the achievement sense) inevitably results from surface learning (in the task sense). Simple memorisation, unreflective association and imposition of tasks cannot but result in poor results. As Ramsden says, commenting on earlier empirical work in this area:

> In the first place, although using a surface approach logically prevents a student from achieving understanding, using a deep approach does not guarantee it. Other things, such as a well-structured knowledge base in the area being studied, are necessary. In other words, surface approaches can never lead to understanding: they are both a necessary and a sufficient condition for poor-quality learning. Deep approaches are a necessary, but not a sufficient condition, for high-quality outcomes.
>
> (Ramsden 2003: 59)

It thus remains to be seen under what conditions deep learning results in good outcomes, although the evidence presented by Ramsden suggests that it can, given for example a 'well-structured knowledge base'. This of course leaves open the question as to how that knowledge base can be acquired. If it was through deep learning, then it would require a further well-structured knowledge base underlying it. Inevitably one arrives at a form of learning which cannot rely on a well-structured knowledge base, because the learner has not yet acquired one. Therefore, on this account, not all successful learning (achievement) could result from deep learning (task). If, however, we strip away the pejorative aspects of the surface learning criteria, then it looks as if we do have testable predictions, because we can now examine whether memorisation, association and external motivation can result in high quality outcomes and, crucially, with what other factors they are associated in order to produce such outcomes.

The use of pejorative and approving language in the description of deep and surface learning conveys the impression that one form of learning is better than another, while at the same time neither giving evidence for such a claim nor saying in what respect it is better. Moreover, some of the claims are not clear enough to be subject to empirical investigation. For example, it is not clear what the phrase 'Focus is on "what is signified"' in Table 5.1 above actually means, and the same applies to 'Organises and structures content into coherent whole'. The formulation of empirical claims about the effectiveness of different kinds of teaching and learning does then need to be considered carefully in order that the nature of the claim being made can be properly understood.

In fact, despite the work that has been carried out on deep and surface learning over a quarter of a century, remarkably little is known about whether or not one form of learning is more effective than the other. Studies cited by Ramsden (2003) suggest that deep approaches may, under certain conditions, result in high quality learning outcomes. We don't know, though, whether non-pejoratively described surface approaches have positive or negative results or under what conditions they are likely to do so. For example, a recent study by Hay (2007) suggests that there is currently no evidence that deep learning leads to achievement in ways that surface learning does not (p. 55), although he accepts the distinction between deep and surface learners and shows that there are measurable differences in outcomes between learners classified as 'deep' and 'surface'. Instead this article proposes that research is needed into the comparative utility of deep and surface learning. The example of research into deep and surface learning is interesting in a number of ways relevant to anyone considering the researching of their own professional work.

First, the research has shown that it is difficult to separate the predictive and prescriptive aspects of claims about deep and surface learning because of a lack of care in formulating the research question.

Second, there has been empirical work that purports to show that there are differences in the approaches to learning of students classified as 'deep' and students classified as 'surface' learners.

Third, claims as to the efficacy of one type of learning as opposed to another are yet to be validated. This may well be due to the difficulty in developing a criterion of relative efficacy that is valid over a range of subject domains. The surface/deep learning distinction remains, therefore, a challenge to the prospective researcher in this area.

Dyslexia in higher education

The final example concerns research into a topic that has received extensive consideration, particularly concerning the reading abilities of children. Dyslexia is thought to be a distinctive condition primarily manifested in difficulties in reading which is, nevertheless, different from other kinds of reading difficulty in being positively associated with other factors such as high performance on IQ tests and difficulties with visual and audial memory. Nonetheless, the precise nature of these associations is elusive and the existence of a distinct condition of dyslexia has for long been challenged or at least subject to serious qualification (e.g. Bryant and Bradley 1985). More recently, building on a quarter century of reported research, Julian Elliott (Elliott and Gibbs 2008) has suggested that the concept of dyslexia is conceptually ill-constructed if not incoherent, and that there is no convincing evidential support for the existence of a distinct condition of dyslexia, as opposed to one of a number of different types of reading difficulty.

If such a condition as dyslexia does indeed exist and if it is difficult to treat and to cure then it should be expected that it would persist into adulthood. For that reason, one would expect a substantial number of students in higher education to be afflicted with the condition. On the other hand, if some kinds of *reading difficulties* are also difficult to treat and cure (and the difficulty may be compounded if there are problems in arriving at an adequate conceptualisation as to what the nature of these difficulties actually is) then we should expect that such difficulties will present themselves amongst higher education students as well. Such considerations will have to be borne in mind when considering research into dyslexia in higher education, such as is to be found in, for example, Simmons and Singleton (2000).

Simmons and Singleton report an experiment carried out on a group of dyslexic students and a control of non-dyslexics which suggests that the former have more difficulties with inferential comprehension than the latter, when controlled for literal comprehension (the ability to report and understand what is written on the printed page). Inferential comprehension involves the ability to infer consequences from certain passages within the text which are not necessarily explicitly set out in the text. The explanation offered is that the difficulties encountered by dyslexics in processing word recognition leave little 'working memory' for inference. It is self-explanatory that such a deficit in comprehension would have significant consequences for the speed and efficiency with which students can read difficult texts, and so is of potential significance in the diagnosis of students with learning difficulties. Unlike the other two areas of research that we previously surveyed, the subject matter dealt with is much less speculative; students with difficulties in reading and comprehension are a phenomenon many if not most lecturers will have encountered.

Simmons and Singleton faced the problem that reading tests designed for children or young people under 18, the great majority were not suitable for the assessment of the reading ability of adults. They therefore designed their own instrument which was designed to be fairly difficult and fairly long, thus suitable for adults engaged in higher education. This is a good example of the subject expertise of two academics (who work in a psychology department) being used to design research addressing a pedagogical problem in their own professional work and designing an instrument specially adapted to the research problem to carry out the work. It is thus a good example of the kind of work that can be achieved and shows, furthermore, the possibilities of dissemination through a recognised and respected refereed journal. The main problem with the evaluation of this work relates not so much to the study itself but to the assumptions concerning the existence of dyslexia which it makes. The authors are carefully agnostic on what interpretation of dyslexia they take to be the most convincing (Simmons and Singleton (2000: 181); they nevertheless take the phenomenon to be a real one insofar as it is predictive of reading difficulties.

However, as Julian Elliott (Elliott and Gibbs 2008) points out, a condition that is a predictor of reading difficulties cannot be assumed to be *dyslexia*, particularly if various and sometimes contradictory assumptions are made about its symptoms. In other words, the dyslexia diagnosis has poor explanatory value, either as an account of the causal mechanisms at work in the development of reading difficulties or as a predictor of reading difficulties in individuals (Lipton 2004). Furthermore, it is a commonplace in the philosophy of science that if a simpler explanation is available out of two competing explanations (or the simplest of more than two), then if it has the same explanatory power as its rivals, then it should be adopted. This does not mean that one should always reject complicated or even inconsistent explanatory frameworks if they provide a good field of testable and potentially useful predictions (Lakatos and Musgrave 1970), but it does suggest that simplicity is, other things being equal, a tie-breaker for the adoption of explanatory frameworks. In this example, the complex and inconsistent explanatory framework of dyslexia has no apparent advantages over an explanatory framework that postulates a continuum of reading difficulties linked in turn to difficulties with phonological awareness and the association of written with spoken symbols (Bryant and Bradley 1985; Elliott and Gibbs 2008).

The example of dyslexia illustrates an important point about higher education research, namely that it is not detached from broader fields of research, debates and research questions in education. Simmons and Singleton's (2000) paper is framed within the 'discourse' of dyslexia, but as such it is potentially misleading, as the design and the findings could equally well have been expressed within an alternative framework. This consideration illustrates one of the difficulties in assessing research into learning and pedagogy in higher education, namely that one needs to understand the background of the research issue in order to formulate an adequate response to it. It may thus often be necessary to conduct further enquiries in order to arrive at a satisfactory evaluation of some particular piece of research. But this illustrates that investigations into pedagogical topics in higher education have to be approached in the same way as investigations anywhere else, namely through an acquaintance with work in the field rather than in a piecemeal fashion. Like all research, detective work is required. In the case of this paper, the penultimate paragraph on page 181 should provide significant clues as to the development of debates in this area, and further enquiries on academic search engines would be needed to supplement the picture.

Expertise

The example just given shows how a properly referenced and scholarly article will provide many of the materials needed for its own proper evaluation. The usual skills employed by academic researchers in any discipline will be transferable *to some extent* to the problems dealt with in research on, for example, pedagogy. However, it is too simple to assume that transfer can just happen. One does need to be attuned to the kind of debate that is happening in this area in order that one can pick up vital signals concerning what to look for. The debate about the existence of dyslexia is a good example of this, as the subject has received extensive media coverage over the last few years, which has included, for example, television programmes involving two significant figures involved in this research, namely Elliott and Snowling. Obviously such programmes need to be treated with caution, but neither are they without value, and they can provide vital clues about what the critical issues are and where to conduct one's own further enquiries.

But the issue of dyslexia is also an interesting one in other respects. First, a great deal of high quality research on the subject has been conducted over the last three decades, so that it is possible to build up a sense of what level of progress has been made in the area. Second, there is a great deal of literature available in professional journals which needs more care in its handling, and where Bassey's (1999) recommendation of conducting an *audit trail* leading from conclusions back to evidence and the way in which the evidence is generated will be critically important. Third there is a great deal of pedagogical material and apparatus related to the diagnosis and treatment of the putative condition of dyslexia, both commercial and non-commercial, whose value needs to be assessed at least partly in the light of the available research evidence. Finally, but not least, there is extensive commercial activity, both profit and non-profit, based on the diagnosis and treatment of dyslexia, whose relationship with the academic research literature is both complex and sometimes controversial. The claims made in this area again need to be evaluated in the light of the best available research.

Essentially we are claiming that in all these areas, which are more or less 'high stakes' in the sense that they critically affect the future prospects of students, the 'gold standard' is the peer-reviewed academic research paper in the area with which you are concerned. There must be an audit of the claims made in professional, pedagogic and commercial sources which leads back to an assessment of the warrant for their claims in the light of known standards for the production of such warrants. And, even then, the term 'gold standard' does not imply that a well-constructed research paper can be taken uncritically. This is not just a matter of closely scrutinising the methodology and methods employed, the nature of the instruments, the level of significance attained, etc., but of getting a sense of the wider debates in which the research and its claims are situated. There can be no substitute for engaging oneself in these wider debates and, in this sense, research into higher education pedagogy is no different from research into anything else.

Exercises

1 Your programme team has asked you to review the literature on the use of ICT as a pedagogical aid in higher education as a prelude to the team formulating a common policy for all members. You have decided to use published articles in the first instance. Outline a review strategy taking the following factors into account:

    1   What aspect of ICT as a pedagogical aid will you focus on?

    2   What kinds of published literature are there – (a) official, (b) commercial, (c) policy, (d) professional, (e) academic refereed. Which will you rely on most and how can they be used to validate each other?

    3   What kind of background research will you need to carry out?

    4   How will you decide which research is worth paying attention to?

    5   How do you select valid pedagogical recommendations from the literature?

    Write two paragraphs outlining the way in which you explain to your colleagues how you have gone about this task and why they can have confidence in your results.

2 Select a research report on an educational topic that interests you. Are the findings sufficiently supported to merit acceptance?

References

Bakhurst, D. (2008) 'Minds, Brains and Education'. *Journal of Philosophy of Education* 42, 3–4: 415–32.

Bassey, M. (1999) *Case Study Research in Educational Settings*. Buckingham: Open University Press.

Bennett, M. and Hacker, P. M. S. (2003) *The Philosophical Foundations of Neuroscience*. London: Routledge.

Bryant, P. and Bradley, L. (1985) *Children's Reading Problems*. Oxford: Blackwell.

Coffield, F., Moseley, D., Hall, E. and Ecclestone, K. (2004) *Learning Styles and Pedagogy in Post 16 Education: A Systematic and Critical Review*. London: Learning and Skills Development Assocation.

Elliott, John (2006) 'Educational Research as a Form of Democratic Rationality'. *Journal of Philosophy of Education* 40, 2: 169–85.

Elliott, Julian and Gibbs, S. (2008) 'Does Dyslexia Exist?' *Journal of Philosophy of Education* 42, 3–4: 475–92.

Hay, D. (2007) 'Using Concept Maps to Measure Deep, Surface and Non-learning Outcomes'. *Studies in Higher Education* 332, 1: 39–57.

Hutchinson, P., Read, R. and Sharrock, W. (2008) *There Is No Such Thing as Social Science*. Aldershot: Ashgate.

Lakatos, I. and Musgrave, A. (1970) *Criticism and the Growth of Knowledge*. Cambridge: Cambridge University Press.

Lipton, P. (2004) *Inference to the Best Explanation*. 2nd edn. London: Routledge.

Ramsden, P. (1988) *Improving Learning: New Perspectives*. London: Kogan Page.

——(2003) *Learning to Teach in Higher Education*. 2nd edn. London: Routledge-Falmer.

Ryle, G. (1949) *The Concept of Mind*. London: Hutchinson.

Saljo, R. (1979) 'Learning About Learning'. *Higher Education* 8, 4: 443–51.

Simmons, F. and Singleton, C. (2000) 'The Reading Comprehension Abilities of Dyslexic Students in Higher Education'. *Dyslexia* 6, 3: 178–92.

Chapter 6

Practitioner research in action

Doing one's own research

Introduction

We have argued that research evidence should be used, where possible, to support teaching and decision making in higher education. We have also argued that both educational and education research are often necessary, since common sense theorising and experiential knowledge may not help us in dealing with problems of practice, especially where opinions differ. For example, some teachers see group work as promoting 'pooled ignorance': others see it as a valuable learning opportunity. Without the evidence provided by well conceived and executed research we must rely on unsupported opinion and anecdote.

However, using research is not simply a matter of applying research findings in an uncritical way, as we have demonstrated in Chapter 5. In this chapter we argue that any research findings, if utilised in one's own work, should be evaluated in the course of one's teaching. This is because findings which pertain for one group of students at a certain time and place may not pertain to a different cohort at a different time and place.

At this point a sceptic might object that given the inevitable contextual variety of teaching (no two cohorts of students are the same) it is impossible to have confidence in education and educational research findings, as applied to our own situations. And if the research is not applicable to other contexts isn't it, in the words of Furlong and Oancea, somewhat 'ephemeral' and of no real significance, however personally worthwhile it has been to the individual researcher? (2005: 13). In other words is educational (and education) research of any real use?

A second objection might be that the recommendation to evaluate research findings in the course of one's teaching is an unrealistic expectation, given the many demands on lecturers' time. These are important objections, since if true they seem to undermine the position that teaching can be a research-informed profession.

In the first part of this chapter we offer a response to these objections. In the second part we suggest some time-efficient ways in which research activities can be integrated with teaching. We also suggest questions that you would be prudent to ask yourself at the planning stage of a practitioner research project, the answers to which should save time later. We give an extended example of a collaborative practitioner research project that one of the authors was involved in, to demonstrate how such a project may be efficiently and effectively organised. We end the chapter with some observations on good practice in reporting one's own practitioner research. But first we reply to the objection that research in education is fruitless since the context is always shifting.

Perspectives on how research gets into policy and practice

There are two misleading pictures that tend to inform our common sense understanding of how significance is achieved. The first is that research findings should be applicable in the way in which natural scientific findings are thought to be. The second is that policy making, or applying research findings, is an unproblematic process involving straightforward and direct application. Let us consider the first claim, that educational or education research should give us cast iron recommendations for practice.

Generalisability

There is a widespread belief that research findings should be generalisable in the way that natural science employs the notion. The assumption is that only explanations that predict events, in a law-like fashion, constitute worthwhile and dependable knowledge. The form of the generalisation is that event X will necessarily occur whenever Y occurs, in standardised conditions. Thus water will always boil at 100°C in standardised conditions, such as air pressure and lack of impurities in the water. The demand is for certainty about what will work.

It has long been understood that it is impossible for education research to produce such laws since the variables involved in educational situations are too numerous. Does this mean that we never have a solid reason for choosing one course of action over another? It is misleading to suppose that only if a strong causal link is demonstrated do we have good reasons to act. In everyday life we do not demand complete certainty before we act. Indeed to do so would be irrational. Imagine someone who refuses to catch the 7.30 train to work because she cannot be sure that the train will appear, even though it is said to be on time, there are no adverse weather or political conditions pertaining. Her behaviour would be irrational. Similarly it would be irrational to ignore well conceived and executed research on the basis that it may not be applicable to the next cohort of students (Barrow and Foreman-Peck 2005).

It may be countered that research findings are still irrelevant to practice. For example let us suppose that large scale research that has produced a generalisation, for example that mentoring students is effective in the majority of cases. We may envisage a situation where, on the basis of this research, mentoring has been introduced and failed. It could be claimed that this shows that research is not really a good basis for action. There are two replies to this. The first is that research findings should be not be taken as infallible guides but as provisional solutions or understandings. They are the best reasons we have for doing something to improve a situation, or the best insight into a situation that is available. The second point is that our orientation to the innovation or insight has to be that of the evaluator. If our students do not benefit from mentoring when others do, then it is useful to know why. We can only find out by producing our own research. At this point it may be countered that this is an unrealistic expectation. We return to this point later.

A frequent complaint raised about practitioner research, as opposed to large scale research, is that it is too small scale and context-specific to justify any generalisations being made. It is frequently argued that one should not generalise from single events. For example, it may be argued that it would be wrong to believe that because this class's essay writing was improved using these methods, the next class's writing will be improved.

But, it may be countered, we do in fact generalise, quite rationally, from singular events, and even form theories based on successive experiences of similarly occurring events. If cohorts of students are of similar composition, in terms of their backgrounds and abilities, we can reasonably expect the next cohort to benefit from similar methods. This is not to say that we are never wrong. The composition of cohorts changes. For instance students coming to university with GNVQs will not necessarily have developed the requisite reading or writing skills. Indeed, it is just such disrupted expectations that often provide the starting point for research. A 'problem' in practice could be defined as a discrepancy between one's expectations and what is actually happening.

In utilising small scale research, the teacher researcher would do well to examine the context in which the research was carried out to see whether the situation depicted approximates her own. The lecturers who researched and published their own studies which are described in Chapter 10, did provide contextual information, enabling others in similar situations to decide on the possible applicability of their findings to their own teaching situations.

Policy making

A second source of sceptical argument about the usefulness of research findings is often a misunderstanding about how they figure in higher level systems decision making, such as at the institutional or national level. We argue that the model of policy making that conceives of researchers as producing objective information about the nature and extent of an educational situation, and demonstrating which policy intervention works, and which can then be applied in other settings, is over simple. Although this model underlies complaints about the quality and usefulness of much educational research, it only has force because it ignores what happens in practice.

Finch points out that many studies have shown the fragmented, incremental and diffuse nature of policy making (Finch 1988: 192). Pratt (2000) argues that, in reality, policy makers often have to act before thorough research findings are available; they are under public pressure to act. Policy makers act on the basis of the research that is already available. Furthermore, policy making demands a much greater range of information than research is able to provide. High level policy makers use commissions, consultations and think tanks (Bridges and Watts 2008). Recent work has demonstrated the potential for more integrative partnerships, where policy makers are involved in decisions about the research and where there is knowledge exchange between researchers and policy makers (Sylva et al. 2007). Nevertheless policy making is carried out in the context of what is politically acceptable or possible.

At an individual or teaching team level, practitioner researchers using and producing research may face analogous micro-political and practical complexities. We have already mentioned differences in groups of students, which may occur because of national policies. Lecturers also have to acknowledge wider constraints on their activities imposed by their institutions. For example, universities may require ethical approval before changes may be tried out, or there may be departmental policies that have to be taken into account. One may be in a department that does not value or encourage pedagogical research activity. Research findings may not be utilised, or carried out, or may simply be ignored because of these adverse conditions, but this does not invalidate them.

Teaching with research in mind

Let us return to the objection that using research and evaluating it in our teaching is an unrealistic expectation. An alternative to seeing research (mistakenly) as providing 'proof' and a counter to the claim that the idea of using research is naively apolitical, and therefore impossible, is to see it as informing, on the basis of systematically derived evidence, deliberation or reflection about what ought to be done. Research evidence may become a useful resource, for individuals or teams in illuminating situations, challenging taken for granted assumptions, suggesting and evaluating alternative teaching interventions. The impact of research may therefore be more or less direct, but nonetheless important, since it is creating knowledge relevant to making decisions (Furlong and Oancea 2005). Our argument is that using research findings to reflect on one's practice may afford a richer understanding of the complexities of the situation, through a more precise conceptualisation and a better informed grasp of how one might go about one's own practice.

One way of describing the way in which research can have significance in teaching is to say that one teaches with research in mind. Reading research which meshes with one's personal professional interests develops our potentiality for bringing about change. Let us return to the example of the value of group talk mentioned at the beginning of this chapter. The research of educational researchers such as Barnes et al. (1969), Barnes (1976), and Britton (1970) demonstrated, through the examination of transcripts of students talking together, the different educational purposes that group talk might serve, and the corresponding tasks that could be usefully set, so that talk avoided becoming 'pooled ignorance'. Although this research was developed with secondary school pupils, and later developed further by other researchers in other contexts (see for example Wegerif and Mercer 1996), the categories of talk developed, and their illustrations, can sharpen thinking about student talk in higher education and suggest criteria for evaluating its worth. It is perhaps easier to see how a teacher familiar with this research could apply such findings in her own classroom, in the sense of being more aware of possibilities for action, having a vocabulary with which to describe it, a rationale for using it and a basis for carrying out her own innovations and evaluation.

Evaluating research through teaching

Having introduced an innovation, on the basis of reading a research report, we may be satisfied if it seems to work. Much of the time we do make this sort of impressionistic judgement about what we are doing and often this kind of impressionistic judgement is all we have time to make and it is an important aspect of a teacher's professionalism that this evaluative activity or reflection is routinely carried out.

In evaluation research, however, the approach must be more systematic. This is because although we believe that we have brought about improvement, the impressionistic evidence is very limited. We have a tendency to believe that which we are convinced of is right. Furthermore it may be that not all students are benefitting. It is not being suggested that a systematic approach is adopted everytime we introduce a change, but it is recommended, if the stakes are high, as in anti-racist teaching discussed in Chapter 1, or if the effects of an innovation are potentially risky, for example teaching that involves homeless persons as clients (see Hartsell and Parker 2000, discussed in Chapter 10). Introducing a patently unpopular teaching method obviously needs careful research and evaluation (see Parsons and Drew in Chapter 10). It is therefore a matter of prudence as well as a matter of adding to a systematic body of pedagogical knowledge to adopt a more systematic approach to at least some of our innovations.

The advantage of carrying out research is that a wider body of evidence will be collected than is normally available in day-to-day activity, and it will be systematically, as opposed to impressionistically, analysed. To the objection that there is no time for this, we suggest that the collection of data or evidence be largely integrated or derived from teaching activities. We discuss some methods of doing this below. At this point it is important to emphasise that the teacher's first obligation is to teach rather than to research. Research activity must not displace or distort teaching activity (see Chapter 9). However, we argue that it is possible to collect evidence that is generated during the course of teaching that enhances the quality of the teaching.

Researching whilst teaching: being systematic

Being systematic is important for the quality of the research where considerations of validity and reliability have to be taken into account. The word 'systematic' means working in an orderly and transparent way so that, in theory, others can easily follow and check what you have done. Being transparent in what one is doing is a condition of the research's reliability, i.e. that sufficient information is provided so that someone else doing the research may come up with a similar result. Thus it is systematic to record in a research diary what activities were carried out with whom, why, and for how long. It is systematic to label tapes, transcripts and other materials such as documents with details of their provenance and other information that will aid retrieval. The analysis of the data also has to be systematic, in the sense that the theoretical framework or model informing the analysis is made explicit and the data is exhaustively analysed. Constructing an audit trail that is checkable by others provides a record for oneself and a means of checking decisions with others (see Miles and Huberman 1984: 245).

A systematic and transparent approach not only allows for checking, but also allows a reader to form a more accurate assessment of the weight of the evidence on which any conclusions are based, i.e. whether the evidence is sufficient and appropriate enough to support the conclusions reached.

A systematic approach will also involve considering issues of validity at the planning stage. Validity is most easily thought of as trustworthiness, and the steps taken to minimise threats to validity can be built in from the start. For example, one can plan an event that involves checking the validity of one's interpretations of, say, one's students' essays by inviting another person to independently code them. (The concept of validity is discussed in greater depth in Chapter 8.) Being systematic need not be time consuming, but it does require a thought out approach to collecting, recording and storing data, before the research commences.

Researching whilst teaching: using assessment as a method for collecting data

Assessment is usually thought of as either formative or summative. Summative assessment is a judgement about what the student has achieved and usually comes at the end point in a course of study. Formative assessment is intended to provide information to the student and the teacher on the student's present state of understanding, and is usually carried out during the course of study in order to influence the teacher's teaching and the student's learning in more productive directions. Assessments therefore are a fruitful source of information about the student's learning which can be used simultaneously to inform teaching decisions and to contribute towards a research inquiry.

Formative assessment need not necessarily be written. Discussion based around various topics can be tape recorded in groups. For example, if one wished to investigate students' understanding of essay writing one could ask them to discuss how and why they would award marks to a selected sample of essays. This is arguably good teaching and good data collection. Another example: students may be asked to write a brief paragraph reflecting on some aspect of their learning, for example independent group work. These reflections may be struc-tured depending on which aspect is being researched. For instance, it may be that students are asked to reflect particularly on their use of the literature. The written responses are useful as data, but they are also useful starting points for discussion about learning in groups.

These examples focus on the skills and processes of learning, but evidence of learning regarding the substantive content of courses can also be collected through formative assessments. For example: asking students to explain ideas in a way that is accessible for a younger age group; asking them to summarise ideas and present them on a slide to the rest of the group; asking them to think up mock examination questions. These activities, if recorded, provide useful infor-mation on current understanding of the content. Taber (2007) also suggests the use of concept maps and short questionnaires.

Other, more time-expensive ways of collecting data can obviously be employed. Meeting students outside of classroom time requires some ethical sensitivity. Students who do not wish to give up their non-class time may feel that they will be less well thought of or disadvantaged in some way. Needless to say, collecting data during the course of one's teaching requires careful planning, and if colleagues are involved, collaboration and co-ordination.

Setting up a practitioner research project

The following is a series of planning decisions and judgements that need to be made when setting up a project. Careful thought at this stage saves time later.

The research focus and question(s)

- What is the substantive topic that you are interested in? (For example, dyslexia, assessment, teaching a particular skill or concept, the introduction of new teaching materials.)
- What is your research question (or set of questions)?
- What research is available on this topic? (There may be none – but if there is you should be read it, also bearing in mind that the literature may cross disciplinary boundaries.)
- Is the research feasible? That is, are you able to collect the data and write it up in the time available? (For example, a study of students' perceptions of a new teaching or assessment method, will provide limited opportunities for data collection if it is introduced too near the end of the course.)
- Is the research question one that would interest others who teach your subject or more generally? (For example, it could be of interest to other academics researching such topics as the transferability of generic skills, or the management of group learning.)
- Is it possible to identify partners with whom you might collaborate?

The approach

- What research approach do you intend to take? (For example, case study, action research or evaluation; see Chapters 3 and 7.)
- Does this approach match the research question? (For example, 'How effective are these teaching materials?' requires an evaluation research design; 'How can I improve the quality of the dialogue in my classes?' requires an action research design.)
- Are the methods of data collection sufficient and appropriate for the research question?
- Are you able to integrate data collection methods into your teaching in such a way that the teaching is enhanced?
- How are you going to build in an element of trustworthiness to give the research credence? (For example, with qualitative data, one might build in inter-coder reliability by asking a colleague to analyse a sample of data.)
- Do you have a system for collecting, ordering and storing data or evidence?

Ethics

The ethical issues involved in practitioner research are discussed in depth in Chapter 9. Here they are listed as a way of flagging up that they need to be considered at the planning stage.

- Who will be involved in the research?
- How will they be involved?
- Who needs to be informed and how will they be informed?
- What permissions do you need to collect?
- What will you do if some students do not give permission for you to involve them in research?
- Does your proposal need to be approved by an ethics committee?
- How and where will you store data?
- What will you do if you have a freedom of information request?
- If colleagues are involved in your research, what reciprocal rights and obligations should be discussed?

Timetabling

It is very useful to timetable in events such as data collection and deadlines for producing draft reports. These dates can be integrated into your teaching timetable.

- When will the project be introduced?
- When will permissions (from participants and ethics committees) be sought?
- When will the innovation (if appropriate) be introduced?

- When will evidence/data be collected, analysed and written up?
- When will you be able to do the necessary reading?
- When and what are the dissemination opportunities?

Much practitioner research is carried out by individuals researching their own practice, sometimes with their students and colleagues as co-inquirers. The following section describes a collaborative practitioner research project, which involved lecturers from different universities. It was funded by the Higher Education Funding Council for England (HEFCE) through the Fund for the Development of Teaching and Learning (FDTL). It is presented here to demonstrate how practitioners can collaborate to investigate an issue of importance to their discipline and of interest to other educators.

An example: enhancing the quality of assessment – the case of dissertations in sociology

Following a critical subject review by the HEFCE, a group of lecturers decided to develop a more robust framework for ensuring the validity and reliability of marking undergraduate dissertations in sociology. The FDTL sponsored a project to identify best practice and to disseminate conclusions to the wider community. The main concerns were to get consensus on the purposes of the dissertation, to raise awareness of the difficulties in ensuring validity and reliability in the assessment of dissertations, and to develop a more robust framework for ensuring consistency of marking.

However, the research question was not fine-tuned until the focus itself had been researched further through discussions and exercises carried out by lecturers from five participating sociology departments. The research problem came to be 'How can consistency in marking be improved across university departments of sociology?' The research was organised around four workshops for the research participants, and a small scale questionnaire survey to all staff and students in three sociology departments was used.

The approach taken was first to evaluate current practice. The marking criteria and guidelines given in the departmental student dissertation handbooks were critically examined by the participants in the first workshop. Problems were noted with these, including the fact that they were often 'unwieldy' and did not provide guidance for students nor were they helpful in ensuring consistent use by markers. Furthermore the criteria had been devised so that the first-class honours criteria formed benchmarks, with the result that third-class honours criteria concentrated on what was missing or inadequate, rather than specifying what merited 'honours degree-worthiness' (Pilkington and Winch 1999).

The participants then developed a new set of criteria, presented and discussed at the first workshop, which they believed were most central in assessing what they agreed should be the learning outcomes of the dissertations.

- There should be a theoretical base to the research question.
- The project should be located in a critical review of the literature.
- The research question should be manageable.
- The quality of the writing should be adequate.
- A logical argument should inform the dissertation.
- The data should be well collected.

In a second workshop, research participants marked a sample of dissertations using the above criteria. The hypothesis that consistency of marking should improve was not borne out due to the fact that markers gave different weights to different criteria (see Pilkington 1999 for a detailed account). After much debate a consensus was arrived at such that two orders of criteria were proposed. The first was a holistic criterion about the 'adequacy of the overall argument, its coherence, integration and use of data, logical progression and critical awareness'. It was concluded that a dissertation cannot be awarded a class mark above that given to this category, whatever the performance of the other criteria (Pilkington and Winch 1999: 13).

Second-order criteria were more specifically attached to elements of the dissertation, such as the research problem, use of theory, literature review, methodology, presentation and expression. It was concluded that a dissertation should achieve a mark for three out of the five second-order criteria that corresponded with the mark achieved on the first-order criterion in order to achieve that mark. When participants marked a further sample of dissertations using first-order and second-order criteria, the degree of consistency improved. The researchers then went on to tackle the problem of different degree classifications. They were able to specify the characteristics of degree class for the first-order criterion ('the argument') and for the second-order criteria (the five elements).

The researchers acknowledged that common understanding of the criteria was possible because they had spent time in discussing them. One of the main conclusions of the research is that a more robust framework for ensuring the consistency of marking depends on developing a common understanding, and that this requires departmental discussion and development work. Written criteria and procedures may be necessary for good practice but they are not sufficient.

This research project is a good example of practitioner researchers addressing a problem of professional interest and importance to others in higher education that has relevance beyond the concerns of the original participants. It has significance because it can be used to inform the deliberations of other groups of practitioners who may be facing similar problems of inconsistency in marking, in similar contexts. It is a useful starting point for the development of similar initiatives in other subject areas.

The report has significant omissions, however, and this is probably due to a format for publication decided upon by the sponsors with dissemination of findings uppermost in their minds. We have touched upon the problem of the incompleteness of many practitioner research reports in Chapter 3. We suggest that in planning and implementing one's own project it is important that one is explicit about one's research approach, ethical issues and one's approach to the literature, even if the dissemination format does not require these to be discussed. Being clear about one's research approach provides guidance for the reader and a conceptual map for you as the researcher. Being clear about the ethical implications of what one is doing is prudent. Being familiar with the literature ensures that one has a sense of the gaps in the research and a better sense of the kind of contribution to professional knowledge one is making. Indeed, the last point is crucial if the research is to be disseminated via an academic publication.

Reporting practitioner research: good practice

The process of doing research differs from the shape it will take when written up. We have already noted that some sponsors or other dissemination sites may not require all the elements involved in doing research well to be reported. The eventual shape of a publication will depend on the intended audience and purpose. However, we suggest that whatever the nature of the publication, it is important to guide the reader into a proper evaluation of the weight that can be put on the findings by pointing out the limitations of the research, so that you do not appear to claim more than is warranted by the evidence.

A possible way of presenting a picture of the data or evidence on which conclusions are reached is to provide a table summarising what you collected, and when, with an indication of its nature, and a discussion of its limitations, for example as shown in Table 6.1.

Other tables can be used to provide information, such as the characteristics of the setting and the participants, and the presentation of results. It should be noted that research can have a relatively poor quality or sufficiency of evidence and still make warranted claims if these are suitably qualified by an acknowledgement of the limitations of the evidence base from which they are inferred. On the other hand, research claims are not warranted where the claims do not logically follow from the evidence, even if the evidence is relatively good. Poor research occurs when the claims made are not warranted by the data.

Table 6.1 Providing a summary table

Date	Data/evidence	Name of group, etc.
25.10.08	Tape recorded class discussions	2nd year group; 20 mins; transcribed
1.11.08	Focus group	2nd year student volunteers; 90 mins; written responses from participants and notes made
2.12.08	Individual written responses – in class	30–c.100 words each
15.1.09	Student presentations	5–10 mins each; written slides and notes

It is also likely that other practitioners will be interested not only in your conclusions and any recommendations made (however tentative), but in the organisation of the research. Practitioner research is arguably strengthened if carried out across sites, since the participants will bring different institutional perspectives; but such research is not easy to manage, so evaluating the success or otherwise of practical arrangements could also make a valuable contribution to our professional knowledge (Foreman-Peck 2005).

One further area is also under-researched. Practitioner research ethics presents particular problems, especially in the management of relationships with colleagues and students who may be co-inquirers. A discussion of any dilemmas encountered and the way in which these were resolved (or not) could also be a contribution to a developing literature.

Exercise

Write an outline draft research proposal using the following headings, and discuss it with an interested colleague.

Working title
Research focus
Research question(s)
Rationale
Literature
Research approach
Data collection methods
Ethical strategy
Timetable
Dissemination strategy

References

Barnes, D. (1976) *From Communication to Curriculum*. Harmondsworth: Penguin Books.

Barnes, D., Britton, J. and Torbe, M. (1969) *Language, the Learner and the School*. Harmondsworth: Penguin Books.

Barrow, R. and Foreman-Peck, L. (2005) *What Use is Educational Research? A Debate*. Impact no. 12. London: Philosophy of Education Society of Great Britain.

Bridges, D. and Watts, M. (2008) 'Educational Research and Policy: Epistemological Considerations'. *Journal of the Philosophy of Education* 42, S1: 42–62.

British Educational Research Association (BERA) (2004) *Ethical Guidelines*. Available at www.bera.ac.uk/publications/pdfs/ethical.pdf.

Britton, J. (1970) *Language and Learning: The Importance of Speech in Children's Development*. London: Pelican Books.

Finch, J. (1988) 'Ethnography and Public Policy', in A. Pollard, J. Purvis and G. Walford (eds) *Education, Training and the New Vocationalism*. Milton Keynes: Open University Press.

Foreman-Peck, L. (2005) *A Review of Existing Models of Practitioner Research*. National Academy of Gifted and Talented Youth. University of Warwick.

Furlong, J. and Oancea, A. (2005) *Assessing Quality in Applied and Practice-based Educational Research: A Framework for Discussion*. Available at www.bera.ac.uk/pdfs/qualitycriteria.pdf.

Hartsell, B. D. and Parker, A. J. (2008) 'Evaluation of Problem-Based Learning as a Method for Teaching Social Work Administration: A Content Analysis'. *Administration in Social Work* 32, 3: 44–62.

Miles, B. M. and Huberman, A. M. (1984) *Qualitative Data Analysis: A Sourcebook of New Methods*. London: Sage Publications.

Pilkington, A. (1999) *Enhancing the Quality of Assessment: The Case of Dissertations in Sociology*. Available at www.c-sap.bham.ac.uk/resources/project_reports/findings/ShowFinding.htm?id (accessed 3.6.08).

Pilkington, A. and Winch, C. (1999) *Assessment Strategies and Standards in Sociology: A Resource Handbook*. Available at www.c-sap.bham.ac.uk/sunject_areas?sociology/fdt/assessment.htm (accessed 3.6.08).

Pratt, J. (2000) 'Research and Policy: A Realist Approach'. *Prospero* 6, 3149.

Sylva, K., Taggart, B., Melhuish, E., Sammons, P. and Siraj-Blatchford, I. (2007) 'Changing Models of Research to Inform Educational Policy'. *Research In Education* 22, 2: 155–68.

Taber, K. S. (2007) *Classroom-based Research and Evidence-based Practice: A Guide for Teachers*. London: Sage Publications.

Wegerif, R. and Mercer, N. (1996) 'Computers and Reasoning Through Talk in the Classroom'. *Language and Education* 10, 1: 47–64.

Chapter 7

Models of practitioner research

Introduction

In Chapter 3, we introduced the distinction, following Robson (2002), between fixed (i.e. pre-set) and flexible (i.e. adaptable) research designs. Of the latter, case study was argued to be the most useful for teachers who are researching their own, or their institution's practices. Case study, as defined by Robson, is a multi-method approach, often thought of as qualitative research, although quantitative data can be used and it can even incorporate a 'fixed design' element, if appropriate. For Robson case study is a 'multimethod enterprise' aimed at developing 'detailed, intensive knowledge about a single "case" or of a small number of related cases' (Robson 2002: 89). It should be noted that the appeal to multi-methods is not a hard and fast rule, but a sound recommendation, since the validity of the research is thereby strengthened. Elliott and Lukes describe *educational* case study more generally, as a 'form of inquiry into a particular instance of a class of things that can be given sufficiently detailed attention to illuminate its educationally significant features' (Elliott and Lukes 2008: 88).

Cases may consist of any 'bounded instance', such as a single student, a cohort of students, a university department, or a set of interactions. The 'boundary' is a conceptual one and occurs or exists in a bounded time frame, such as the academic year. The 'case' is always situated in a natural (i.e. non-laboratory) setting, such as a classroom. The context is an important factor in understanding case study research. Individual cases are embedded in social practices, places and systems, and these may have unique features. This means that generalisations, as we saw in Chapter 6, cannot be made in a way that is possible with quantitative research. This point is discussed further in the present chapter.

The term 'case study' can be confusing since it is also used to refer to a range of texts, also called case studies. Educational case study should not, for instance, be confused with vignettes used for teaching, training or staff development purposes. Educational case studies are intensively researched, ideally employing mutimethods. Chapter 10 presents four examples. The present chapter discusses the most common types of case study, with an emphasis on action research, as this is likely to be the approach most often employed.

As we noted previously, educational research is motivated and distinguished by the intention to improve educational practices, and it is usual to distinguish different styles of case study according to the way in which this intention is specified. We may intend to gain an in-depth understanding of an educational practice or situation, or we may intend to introduce a change, or to evaluate the success or otherwise of an intervention. These distinctions simply serve to identify the main concern of the researchers in the study. They do not serve to impose a 'fixed' pattern on the conduct or content of particular studies. Case study reports may take on a wide variety of different genres, from descriptive, to biographical, to technical (see Bassey 1999, for a suggested typology). Case studies may also display a *mix* of intentions. For example researchers may intend to bring about change, but they may first need to study a situation in more depth in order to understand the problem, or the problem may be already well substantiated. In each case the final case study will take a different 'shape'. Robson makes the point that case study is not a 'flawed experimental design; it is a fundamentally different research strategy with its own designs' (Robson 2002: 180).

In Chapter 6 we introduced some questions that needed to be considered at the planning stage before carrying out research. In this chapter we look at the elements of design that have to be considered in any research approach, fixed or flexible. These are:

- the purpose(s)
- the research questions
- theory
- the sample (or participants)
- ethical issues
- validation.

In this chapter and the next we discuss the research design elements listed above in the most common versions of case study design: educational action research, descriptive educational case study and educational evaluation. The ethics of practitioner research is discussed in depth in Chapter 9. In this chapter the first section describes some general features of action research and is followed by a section with more detail of different versions. The third section explains descriptive educational case study research drawing on the influential work of Stenhouse. The fourth section deals with evaluation research and distinguishes it from reflective practice.

Educational action research case study: general features

Action

Action research is often employed when there is a perceived need for change, especially at an individual or institutional level. As the name implies, 'research' and 'taking action' are linked. The way in which 'action' is theorised, however, differs in various versions of action research; it may be seen as applying and testing pre-existing theories, (technical action), or it may be seen as gaining an in-depth understanding of the meanings of others who are part of the practice problem (practical or interpretative action), or it may be envisaged as awareness of oppressing and disempowering ideologies, requiring political action. Before considering these various interpretations of action research, we discuss some general features which apply to all three.

Problem focused – 'how to' questions

Action research is always addressed to problems that arise in practice. A 'problem' can be thought of as a discrepancy between the desired effect of an action or policy and the actual effect. For instance it maybe that the assessment policy endorsed by your department to make assessment fairer and more transparent to students is proving unworkable, or, on a more personal level, it may be that you are not sure of the best way to meet the learning needs of students with disabilities, which you would like to do. These problems can be expressed as practical or 'how to' problems. We can reformulate the concerns mentioned above as research questions, namely 'How can we amend the assessment policy so that it fulfils our objectives and values?' and 'How can I find out more about students with disabilities and alter my practice so that they are not disadvantaged?'

Some researchers prefer to ask 'appreciative' rather than critical questions. They argue that it is better to ask positive questions as a starting point, focusing on 'the best of what is' and to envisage positive change (Ludema et al. 2006: 158). Clearly this is a matter of judgement. In some situations people are not willing to admit that there is a 'problem', or it would be unproductive to suggest that there is one, for example, with a badly behaved class of fifteen-year-old boys. Similarly, others may prefer to talk about a 'puzzle' in order to avoid the sometimes felt criticism contained in the word 'problem'.

Who defines the problem?

Lewin (1946) is often credited with the invention of action research. He saw it as a way of promoting democracy, and there has remained a strong commitment to democratic ideals by action research theorists. This means in practice that the *participation* of those engaged in a problem is necessary. This involvement is especially important at the stage of problem identification and planning an action, both for moral and pragmatic reasons. Morally, participation is necessary, since the lives of others will be altered by an intervention, and pragmatically, an intervention that does not involve the full involvement of participants is unlikely to succeed. Participants in research, however, are not just those who are involved in an active sense. The British Education Research Association's *Ethical Guidelines* for educational researchers state that 'participants in research may be the active or passive subjects of such processes as observation, inquiry, experiment or test. They may be collaborators or colleagues in the research process or they maybe simply part of the context' (BERA 2004: 4). This point has important consequences for the conduct of research and is discussed in Chapter 9.

Problems emerge in different ways. Sometimes they result from reflection on our own experiences in teaching and the focus will be our own development. Sometimes they feel imposed or 'top down' due to changes in the environment beyond our control. Nevertheless, however they emerge, they will involve the lives of others.

Working with others: collaboration and cooperation

Action research theorists argue that collaboration is a necessary element in action research design, i.e. that a project *cannot be* action research unless there is some form of collaboration (e.g. Kemmis and McTaggart 1988; Somekh 2006). However, the concept of collaboration is generally invoked without much analysis. In practice, collaborative relationships can take different forms and carry different expectations and responsibilities. It can be taken to imply that all participants in the research should take part in the decision making and in problem identification, implementation and data collection and evaluation. This comprehensive form of collaboration, involves participation at every stage of the research with each person becoming a co-inquirer, and accepting equal responsibility for the research (although this does not mean that all participants need to be 'doing the same' (Cohen et al. 2007)).This comprehensive form of collaboration is usually designated 'participant action research' (PAR) and is often used in contexts other than schools or universities, such as banks, trade unions or museums (see e.g. the PAR case study in a bank by Elden 1991). In its overtly political use, PAR is associated with the work of Freire (1970) and Torres (1992).

However, in other collaborative configurations, the participants may not have the knowledge, experience or authority to define a problem, or to contribute as equals to all stages of the research. Here responsibility for the research lies with an individual rather than the group. An example of this would be the action research carried out by Harris into his teaching of history writing with groups of students. The students were fully informed participants, who voluntarily contributed their thinking, and provided data in the course of their learning, but their collaborative activity was constrained by their position as students. As students, for example, they could not have attended examination moderation meetings (Harris and Foreman-Peck 2001). It would probably be more accurate to say that the students *cooperated* with his research.

Between the extremes of full participation and cooperation there are other configurations. The responsibility for the definition of the problem and the carrying out of tasks, such as data collection, analysis, reflection, and final writing up, will differ according to individual circumstances. For example, some action researchers may be able to use the services of a research assistant or consultant to whom the collection of data, analysis and writing up are delegated. One would expect, however, that given the democratic spirit of action research, all participants would have a say in the formulation of the problem, possible courses of action and in reflection on the evidence used for evaluation.

Action research with children under 18 years, and vulnerable adults, may present particular communicative challenges, which need careful consideration. Working with university-age students also presents challenges, but probably more to do with the differential statuses between teachers and taught, than difficulties in communication. Students may feel 'compelled' to cooperate in an action research project, since they may fear that it will offend their tutor not to do so, and thus would be detrimental to their interests not to take part. This presents a real challenge for the design of any action research, since informed and voluntary involvement is necessary, not only ethically, but also in terms of the validity of the data obtainable and the quality of the interaction that is possible.

Insiders and outsiders: some ethical matters

It should be clear by now that action research is carried out by practitioners who are professionally accountable for a situation which is problematic. Action researchers are therefore invariably 'insiders', that is, in Cochran-Smith and Lytles' (1993) terminology, 'workers' involved in the site of the research. Action research is always focused on a practice problem in which the practitioner researcher is reflecting upon and making decisions about their own practice, or their institution, and for which they are accountable.

'Outsiders' may be involved as consultants, research assistants, or in an advisory capacity. They may feel a sense of responsibility for the success of the study, but it is the practitioners themselves who 'own' the problem. Acting in the role of an outsider is tricky in that they must be neither directive nor non-directive. The problem to be researched may be helpfully reformulated or clarified by an 'outsider', or they may draw attention to matters that have not been considered. But the practitioner researchers do have to acknowledge that it *is* a problem, and that it is relevant and important to them.

For insiders, the involvement of others is essential, and the relevance and importance of a topic to them is clearly important. The action researcher needs to be careful and skilful in relating to colleagues, students and managers, especially as action research is not generally well understood. The demands on peoples' time, their degree of involvement, issues about the ownership of data and ownership of possible publications need to thought about and discussed in advance. Being able to anticipate any adverse consequences for other participants is also a moral responsibility. Where the participants are adults, equal in institutional status and each potentially able and qualified to contribute on an equal footing, the workload, direction of the research and the authorship of any publications can be negotiated in advance.

Ownership issues may differ with the different statuses of participants. For example in the action research case study reported by Harris and Foreman-Peck (2001), the appreciation of the problem (how the teaching of history writing could be mproved) was necessarily limited, as we have remarked. The students may be interested in the research, but they are not in a position to decide whether it is in their best interests. In this case it seems appropriate to speak of a lead researcher who makes decisions with and for the group, on the basis of discussion and evidence, in their best interests. University-age students are also in an unequal relationship with tutors, in certain respects. Teachers' and lecturers' primary respon-sibility is for teaching. It seems uncontroversial to insist that, as with younger students, whatever is carried out is justifiable as being in this cohort's best interests and, of course, with their fully informed agreement.

Critical friends

The action research group, as we have seen, may be made up of people occupying the same or different positions in an organisation. Outside of this group, other people may be involved in different roles. For instance, the action research group may decide to employ another group as advisors or 'critical friends'. Chosen for their experience or expertise, this group can offer advice about the direction of the research, point to relevant literature or resources, and help think through any ethical issues arising in the course of the research. They may also critically evaluate the research, challenge assumptions, and comment on the research's rigour and credibility. It is prudent to employ a group of this kind, if possible, to provide another perspective, in any action research project. On award-bearing courses in higher education for teachers, lecturers and other professionals, col-leagues as well as supervisors may fulfil this function (see e.g. McNiff and Whitehead 2006).

The action research spiral of steps

While not prescribing particular data collection methods, action research does follow a cycle of steps, first described by Lewin (1946). These have been elaborated upon by various writers on action research (for a useful summary see Cohen et al. 2007: 304–9), but the basic idea is that the following steps will be discernible:

1 problem specification or reconnaissance;
2 planning an intervention;
3 implementing and monitoring the intervention;
4 evaluating its success or otherwise;
5 revising the research problem and repeating the cycle if necessary.

Although the above steps should be discernible, it does not follow that an equal amount of time will be spent on each. It may be for example that step 1 involves several episodes of data collection and reflection ('research action') in order to feel confident that the problem has been satisfactorily specified and looked at from all points of view. In the context of academic work, step 1 will also involve reading the literature, not only to find out what is already published, but also to enable the development of relevant theory, whether this is 'grounded' or utilised in a fixed design. In many work contexts, the literature will include legislation and government policies which entail obligations, constraints, or challenges. Understanding and theorising the problem may be a major challenge, but it is a necessary preliminary to planning an intervention.

Step 2, the planning an intervention stage, needs to include not only a plan of action (what will de done, by whom and when) but the criteria and/or objectives by which the intervention will be evaluated as a success or not. It should also contain an hypothesis, which may be implicitly or explicity expressed. The form of reasoning is as follows: if we do action X, which we have good reasons to believe will result in an improvement, then Y should follow. At step 4, the judgement is made about whether Y did follow. If it did not then either the problem is reformulated or a new plan devised (step 5).

It should be emphasised that the implementation ('implementation action') phase (step 3) requires careful monitoring and data collection, in order that the implementation can be evaluated. This requirement is sometimes overlooked, rendering the evaluation stage impossible in any systematic way.

The discussion above has pointed to general features in various versions of action research found in the literature, and pointed to some of the ethical and practical challenges in working with others. In the section that follows we highlight the differences in the various perspectives on action research promoted by theorists. While they are presented here as discrete versions, with distinct epistemologies, elements of each can be found to varying degrees in published reports of action research inquiries (for a discussion see Foreman-Peck and Murray 2008).

Versions of action research

Action research as practical philosophy

Elliott's model of action research is informed by the view that teachers should realise their educational values, and those of their community, in practice (Elliott 2007). Thus it is a form of practical philosophy; it requires awareness on the part of practitioners of the values that inform their educational actions. This necessitates deliberation about the aims of education and the values inherent in aspects of education, such as teaching methods and assessment systems. These are likely to differ in institutions with different missions and between subjects. For instance, an IT lecturer in a vocationally oriented university, is more likely to value the idea of 'employability' than, say, a philosophy lecturer in a traditional university who works with ideas of initiation into a cultural heritage. We say 'more likely', because it is perfectly possible to find examples of vocationally oriented philosophy lecturers and traditionally oriented IT lecturers. But in either case, the point is that educational values will be pertinent to what is to count as a 'problem' in practice. The emphasis on the practitioner researcher's aims and values gives this version of action research a strongly individualistic and self-evaluative direction. In a later work, however, Elliott argues that action researchers should take into account systemic factors and include the values and aims of other 'stakeholders' in any deliberations (Elliott 1993).

A possible consequence of such reflections may mean that a teacher finds herself at odds with the prevailing educational situation. A discrepancy between what is the case and what ought to be the case is the starting point for action and the aim is for a better alignment of values and action, where this is possible and prudent (for an example see the action research report of Brearley and Van-Es 2002 into their teaching of speaking and listening).

Technical action research

Technical action research is directed not towards foregrounding values realisation, but effectiveness. It is motivated by a desire to make practices more effective, possibly through the application and testing of research findings generated by other researchers, and an emphasis on outcome measures. Two objections are frequently made to this kind of action research. First, that it is not a good way to develop teacher knowledge. It is argued that professional knowledge is essentially moral and that technical action research does not concern itself with the morality of the practice itself (e.g. Carr 2003). We have criticised the view that teaching is solely a moral endeavour in Chapter 4 and will not repeat the arguments here.

The second objection is based on the form of thought that is believed to underpin technical rationality. It is claimed that it involves an instrumental or means–end form of thinking. This way of thinking sees the *means* by which we do something as morally neutral, in the way that a tool is not of itself 'moral' or 'immoral', although the use to which it is put may be. In teaching, on the contrary, the means or methods *are* moral or immoral, since the ends we hope to achieve cannot be separated from them. This can be easily appreciated if we consider the attempt to indoctrinate someone. Our methods will exclude giving students the right to think for themselves or to criticise. A related objection is that technical ways of thinking can only report whether a method achieves its end or not; they cannot illuminate *why* something may 'work' or not.

Given that action research is designed to improve practices, this critique of technical action research may seem to some to be rather perverse. Surely, they might object, the point of such research is to improve practices in the sense of making them more effective?

We may agree with the critics of technical action research that interventions which seem to work, but do not provide understanding of why they work, are problematic. For example, research which showed an increase in students' scores associated with a certain method of teaching would not be helpful unless it was (a) connected to a satisfactory explanatory theory, and (b) morally and educationally acceptable. However, case study research, as we have explained, is unlikely to face this objection, since it is (ideally) a multimethod approach. This means that any instrumental explanation will be qualified by non-instrumental explanations. For instance, knowing that a method 'works' using an outcome measure may be balanced by knowing why it didn't work for certain students, and this may only be elicited through interviews where their views are asked for. The way in which students interpret the requirements of a new method may differ, for example. This may well be the case where students come from different cultural backgrounds with different educational rules and norms. To take another example; research, such as a survey, that showed that certain departments produced consistently better results than others but offered no insights into why this might be so, is not likely to be useful, by itself, to practitioners. But it could serve as an indication of where to look for further for explanations. Single 'fixed' designs have a use but only as part of a multimethod approach. We argue that it is a false move to claim that a concern with 'effectiveness' within a case study is never justified (for an example of an action research study concerned with 'effectiveness' using a multimethod approach, see Jennings 2002).

However, we need not deny that many problems in education are not about effectiveness at all. Where the ideological thinking of an educational situation is in question a different emphasis is needed. One of the present authors taught in a secondary school where the teacher in charge of the library allowed white boys to take out three books and black boys two. Clearly this is not a technical or effectiveness problem, but one of racist attitudes and unjust practices. The following section describes a version of action research which explicitly aims at researching issues of this kind.

Action research as critical social science

Whereas the technical version of action research aims at producing causal explanations and predictive generalisations (in the sense which we have argued in Chapters 6 and 8) and the practical or interpretative tradition aims at uncovering the differing meanings actors give to a situations, critical action research is focused on exposing false beliefs about practice, and taking prudent action to remedy them. In the example above, there was a clear contradiction between valuing each student as an equal member of the community and the actual practices in place.

Action research as critical social science is directed towards the emancipation of participants from unjust situations. This is achieved through dialogue with participants in the research, who explore the historical antecedents and political contexts of their problems, in order to clarify their own ideas about just practice (for an example in the context of nursing see Titchen 1997). For Carr and Kemmis (1986) and others in the critical social science tradition, the underlying epistemology is constructivist: knowledge is developed by a process of active construction and reconstruction by those involved in the research. Unlike the other two versions of action research, all the participants are co-inquirers. This is because the process of the research involves the group in dialogue and reflection, testing their beliefs against the evidence. This model is more likely to be critical of institutional or national policies that prevent the realisation of the groups' ideas ('theorems') about education and the way it is conducted, whereas the interpretative version is more likely to focus on self-evaluation and the technicist on interventions 'that work'.

Clearly, choosing a version of action research depends on the kind of research question one is asking. However, as we remarked earlier in the chapter, the versions are not, nor need be, discrete in practice. Researching an unjust practice still involves an implementation and an evaluation of its effectiveness, if it is to be action research.

Action learning

A form of inquiry which is easily confused with action research is action learning. This is a form of practice based leaning, in which a group of people, usually numbering between four and seven, meet to explore their own work based problems, through shared reflection on their projects. It is akin to action research in that it shares the same basic premise, which Revans summed up as 'there is no learning without action and no (sober and deliberate) action without learning' (quoted in McGill and Beatty 1992: 174). It differs from action research in that its participants do not aim to contribute to a public body of professional knowledge, and are therefore not concerned in the same way with issues of rigour, reliability and validity. Put another way, action learning does not necessarily employ 'rigorous methods for validating evidence in support of a claim to knowledge' (McNiff and Whitehead 2006: 256).

Descriptive educational case study

Educational case study can, as we have mentioned, take various forms, and writers have employed different classifications (see Bassey 1999: 27–30, for a review). Educational case study is indebted to the work of Stenhouse, who thought through the major epistemological problems associated with studying singular cases (1978, 1984). The case study model drawn on here is that which was developed by Stenhouse, for whom the aim of educational case study is to study and portray a situation or phenomenon in depth, in order to better understand and judge it. Stenhouse argued that educational case study was akin to writing a history: just as historians work from archives that are in the public domain, so do educational researchers. In educational case study the 'case', like the history, is constructed from a selection of materials (the case record) extracted from the full set of available materials (the case data/data archives). In educational case study, the case data might be partially 'found' (for example pre-existing information on examination results, and other documents) and partially constructed by the researcher from data collected in the field. The research methods are predominantly interviews, and non-participant observation, using recording methods such as audio and video tape recordings. In the case of a teacher researching her own class, participant observation might also be used. Unlike action research case study, action is not taken as part of the research. The researcher though, may produce a set of recommendations for practice.

Educational case study should be distinguished from ethnographic case study, which is undertaken by cultural and sociological anthropologists. This form of research is generally not suitable for practitioner researchers for several reasons. First, it involves lengthy immersion by the researcher in the lives and culture of the subjects they are researching, as an 'outsider'. Educational case study differs in that even where the teacher is not also the researcher, the researcher is not (usually) a 'stranger' to the site of the research. Teachers and researchers cannot help but have relevant 'accumulated experiences' (a 'general second record') of educational situations (Stenhouse 1984: 231).

Second, Stenhouse argued that for case study claims to be verifiable, there should be a separation between evidence or data, and the researcher's interpretation: data should not be interpreted at the point of collection, as is the case in anthropological methods. The separation of evidence and the researcher's interpretation allows knowledge claims to be checked by others, using the case records, and if necessary the full data archive.

Stenhouse argued that the way in which case study findings generalised to other contexts was not in terms of whether the 'case' was (statistically) representative of a class of people, but in terms of the reader's judgement about whether they could discern a relevant similarity between cases. In other words cases could provide retrospective generalisations, as opposed to predictive laws. They can inform professional judgement by alerting one to similarities between past and present cases. They have the potential to provide insight into new cases, and in this way build practitioners' judgements (Stenhouse 1978).

Grounded theory case study

It has already been mentioned that in educational research pre-existing empirically derived or a priori theories are not always available. The grounded theory approach, originally advocated by Glaser and Strauss (1967), is very attractive to practitioner researchers in that it allows for new theory to emerge. It is particularly suited to qualitative data, such as interviews. It involves progressive focusing, that is, a small amount of data is first collected, and then an emerging hypothesis is developed by further data collection and analysis. Sampling, in the grounded theory approach, is always purposive, so that more information can be gathered to enable the further development of conceptual categories. Data analysis in the grounded theory approach is by the constant comparative method (see Robson 2002: 193–94, for an excellent summary).

A problem with the approach is the claim that it is possible to collect data in the 'field' with no theoretical concerns. This would be an impossibility, as most human perception is theory laden, that is we cannot perceive something unless we have the relevant conceptual structures. For example, we could not perceive a group of people as a 'class', unless we had the concept 'class' and other relevant concepts such as 'student', 'teaching', 'learning'. However, it is possible to be self-conscious or reflexive about one's theories and to approach data collection with broad orientating concepts in mind, which enables non-preconceived categories to emerge. Indeed, it is hard to know how one would not do so, given that one has to design research instruments, such as interview schedules. Glaser and Strauss (1967), in later work, disagreed about the way in which grounded theory should develop and recommended different schemas for data analysis (see Kelle 2005 for a useful summary).

Evaluation research explained: two basic ones; how they differ from Schön's reflective practice model

A further model of research that is particularly suited to teachers is evaluative case study. Generally speaking evaluations are concerned with judging the success or failure of an intervention. Evaluation differs from 'assessment' in that it is not focused on an individual student's success or failure, but has a wider scope. In educational research, evaluation typically focuses on the efficacy of teaching methods, materials or whole teaching programmes, which have not been introduced in response to a practitioner defined problem, as in action research, but have come about in other ways. For instance a new textbook that looks good, or a new assessment method that seems more appropriate, might be the topic of an evaluation at classroom level. At a systems level, a new way of inducting students into university study might be the topic of interest. This kind of evaluation should be distinguished from course or module evaluations which are carried out as a matter of routine in most universities. These are usually standardised, aimed at measuring student satisfaction, and are intended as a quality assurance measure. Evaluation for research purposes is, in contrast, always 'tailor made' to answer specific research questions.

A further distinction ought also to be made between evaluations carried out by practitioners addressed to their questions and commissioned evaluations, where the aim is to provide information to policy makers who may have to make decisions about continued funding, as for example in evaluating the success of a degree programme. Where jobs, reputations and careers are at stake, this kind of evaluation can be highly sensitive, and the ethical dimension has to be very carefully thought through.

Summative and responsive or formative evaluation

There are two basic approaches that practitioners may adopt, depending on one's purposes. Where the evaluation is intended to show success or failure, the evaluation will be judged by the outcomes the intervention is meant to bring about. For instance, a programme might have been designed in order to help graduates get graduate level jobs. Success may be measured by an increase in the number of students getting such jobs, over previous years. Summative, or outcomes-focused evaluation, has been criticised as being of limited help to teachers, since the news that an intervention works, or does not, is of little use by itself. Teachers and others need to know why and how something worked: that a programme has been successful in the past does not of itself provide explanation or illumination. This is not to say that such work is valueless, merely that it should be supplemented. Consider another example: suppose that an analysis of examination results showed that students from a certain ethnic background performed consistently poorly over a number of years on a certain type of assessment. This is an interesting finding but it does not of itself indicate any specific action. Teachers are interested in actionable knowledge.

An alternative to summative evaluation is responsive or formative evaluation. Many evaluations are concerned not only with the outcomes, but also with explaining why and how an intervention worked, whether it is efficient. Evaluations can be designed to help in the development of the intervention itself. In responsive or formative evaluation, the design of the intervention is not fixed. The intervention is evaluated at various points and information is fed back from the researcher to the participants in order to re-direct the intervention in a more profitable direction. Success criteria might still consist of some quantifiable measures, but the focus of the evaluation is more on developing and understanding the intervention, and multimethods will be used.

Schön and reflective practice

How does research evaluation differ from reflective practice? In Schön's (1987) reflective practitioner model the practitioner takes decisions, in action, based on her evaluation of a situation and implements change that is in line with her particular 'ends in view'. We argued in Chapter 2 that this kind of evaluation is co-terminus with professional judgement.

In professional judgement, we bring together our subject knowledge, our applied subject knowledge, our pedagogic knowledge, our practical knowledge, knowledge of the setting, and our accumulated experiences in order to understand and evaluate the present situation. Acts of professional judgement, or, in Schön's phrase, 'knowing-in–action', occur throughout one's professional life and large parts of it may be spontaneous and tacit.

We become aware of our professional knowledge when we face a problem or an unexpected situation and have to deliberate, as Schön said, in order to decide what to do. This usually takes place away from the site, after the event, in a quiet moment. We may reflect *on action*, that is we may think back on what we have done in order to discover how our 'knowing-in–action', or judgement, may have contributed to an unexpected outcome, and as a result we may revise our thinking.

Research evaluation differs from 'reflection-on-action' in that it involves a deliberately designed strategy to answer questions, systematic data collection, and verification, as opposed to relying on our memory of an event. However, the starting point for a research evaluation may well originate in our appreciation, either on the spot, or later, that there is a problem and we are dissatisfied with our current knowledge and understanding. The aim of all case study research is to build professional wisdom in the sense of 'rapid, responsive interpretation of the unpredicted' (Stenhouse 1978: 29).

Exercises

1 Consider the following research questions. Which case study approach would you consider the most appropriate to use and why?

- How can I improve my teaching of X?
- How can I be sure that this method of assessment is fair to all students?
- Is this textbook better than the alternatives available?
- What is the experience of students from my discipline working in colla-boration with students from different disciplines?

2 Discuss with a colleague an idea for a case study. What would be your purpose? What case study model would you adopt?

References

Bassey, M. (1999) *Case Study Research in Educational Settings*. Buckingham: Open University Press.

Brearley, S. and Van-Es, C. (2002) 'One Mouth, Two Ears', in O. McNamara (ed.) *Becoming an Evidence-Based Practitioner: A Framework for Teacher-Researchers*. London and New York: RoutledgeFalmer.

British Educational Research Association (BERA) (2004) *Ethical Guidelines*. Available at www.bera.ac.uk/publications/pdfs/ethical.pdf.

Carr, D. (2003) *Making Sense of Education: An Introduction to the Philosophy and Theory of Education and Teaching*. London: RoutledgeFalmer.

Carr, W. and Kemmis, S. (1986) *Becoming Critical: Education, Knowledge and Action Research*. London: Falmer.

Cochran-Smith, M. and Lytle, S. L. (1993) *Inside/Outside: Teacher Research and Knowledge*. New York: Teachers College Press, Columbia University.

Cohen, L., Manion, L. and Morrison, K. (2007) *Research Methods in Education*. London: Routledge.

Elden, M. (1991) 'Sharing the Research Work: Participative Research and Its Role Demands', in P. Reason and J. Rowan (eds) *Human Inquiry: A Sourcebook of New Paradigm Research* (ch. 22). Chichester: John Wiley and Sons.

Elliott, J. (1993) 'What Have We Learned from Action Research in School-Based Evaluation?' *Educational Action Research Journal* 1, 1: 175–86.

——(2007) *Reflecting Where the Action Is*. London: Routledge.

Elliott, J. and Lukes, D. (2008) 'Epistemology as Ethics In Research and Policy: The Use of Case Studies'. *Journal of the Philosophy of Education* 42, S1: 87–119.

Foreman-Peck, L. and Murray, J. (2008) 'Action Research and Policy'. *Journal of the Philosophy of Education* 42, S1: 145–63.

Freire, P. (1970) *Pedagogy of the Oppressed*. Harmondsworth: Penguin.

Glaser, B. G. and Strauss, A. L. (1967) *The Discovery of Grounded Theory*. Chicago: Aldine.

Harris, R. and Foreman-Peck, L. (2001) 'Learning to Teach History Writing: Discovering What Works'. *Educational Action Research Journal* 9, 1: 97–109.

Jennings, S. (2002) 'Helping Weak Readers Up the Reading Ladder', in O. McNamara (ed.) *Becoming an Evidence-Based Practitioner: A Framework for Teacher-Researchers*. London and New York: RoutledgeFalmer.

Kelle, U.(2005) '"Emergence" vs. "Forcing" of Empirical Data? A Crucial Problem of "Grounded Theory" Reconsidered'. *Qualitative Social Research* 6, 2: art. 27.

Kemmis, S. and McTaggart, R. (1988) *The Action Research Planner*. Geelong, VIC: Deakin University Press.

Lewin, K. (1946) 'Action Research and Minority Problems'. *Journal of Social Issues* 2, 4: 34–46.

Ludema, J. D., Cooperrider, D. L. and Barrett, F. J. (2006) 'Appreciative Inquiry: The Power of the Unconditional Positive Question', in P. Reason and H. Bradbury (eds) *Handbook of Action Research* (ch. 13). London: Sage.

McGill, I. and Beatty, L. (1992) *Action Learning: A Guide for Professional, Management and Educational Development*. London: Kogan Page.

McNiff, J. and Whitehead, J. (2006) *All You Need to Know about Action Research*. London: Sage.

Robson, C. (2002) *Real World Research: A Resource for Social Scientists and Practitioner-Researchers*. Oxford: Blackwell.

Schön, D. (1987) *Educating the Reflective Practitioner: Towards a New Design for Teaching and Learning in the Professions*. San Francisco: Jossey Bass.

Somekh, B. (2006) *Action Research: A Methodology for Change and Development*. Buckingham: Open University Press.

Stenhouse, L. (1978) 'Case Study and Case Records: Towards a Contemporary History of Education'. *British Educational Research Journal* 4, 2: 21–39.

——(1984) 'Library Access, Library Use and User Education in Academic Sixth Forms: An Autobiographical Account', in R. G. Burgess (ed.) *The Research Process in Educational Settings: Ten Case Studies*. London: Falmer Press.

Titchen, A. (1997) 'Creating a Learning Culture: A Story of Change in Hospital Nursing', in S. Hollingsworth (ed.) *International Action Research: A Casebook for Educational Reform*. London: Falmer Press.

Torres, C. A. (1992) 'Participatory Action Research and Popular Education in Latin America'. *International Journal of Qualitative Studies in Education* 5, 1: 51–62.

Chapter 8

Standards in practitioner research

Introduction

We have been suggesting that case study is the most practicable and useful form of practitioner research, even though the quality of such case studies, often written by busy practitioners, is sometimes questioned (Foreman-Peck and Murray 2008). We have addressed the issue of quality standards for practitioner research in Chapter 3. Here we discuss in more depth the issue of verification, that is, the means by which practitioner researchers can present their research as credible and trustworthy. This is important for the users of research: practitioners whose work may be informed by the research and researchers who may wish to build upon the findings of others. Reassurance is needed that the findings or recommendations proposed are sufficiently sound to be taken seriously.

Verification is, however, no simple matter. In Chapter 5, for instance, the notion of providing an 'audit trail' was introduced, which would allow an 'auditor' to check claims made in the case study, with references to the case record (Bassey 1999: 77). Bassey's suggestion that an auditor's certificate of assurance from a named academic be attached to published case studies has not been taken up by researchers and editors, and published case studies appear without the case record for obvious reasons of space. Quantitative data are more easily presented in tables than qualitative evidence. Suggestions for a measure of transparency have been made in Chapter 6 in the form of a table summarising details of the nature and amount of data and evidence that any conclusions or recommendations are drawing on. A great deal of trust must be placed in the researcher. Research training is important here and in the context of award-bearing courses, such as the Certificate in Higher Education, and in departmental reviews of research, certain standards for the validation of practitioner research ought to be insisted on. McNiff and Whitehead usefully describe the role of a validation group, whose purpose is to scrutinise colleagues' data or evidence, consider knowledge claims and question weaknesses in internal validity (McNiff and Whitehead 2006: 159–62). Articles for publication in academic journals should be subjected to rigorous anonymous peer review.

Given the difficulty of publishing the case study 'record', the lack of a national archive of materials (such as would be available to a historian), and the impossibility of the scientific replication of 'findings' in most (but not all) cases, we might ask whether case study knowledge claims are of use to anyone else beside those carrying them out to develop their personal professional wisdom. What makes any findings, conclusions or actions from case study research valid or trustworthy? A sceptic may question whether a case study accurately describes and explains a state of affairs. Or if we are concerned with evaluating 'what works', the sceptic may ask, how do we know that it was the intervention that produced the outcome and not something else? And in the case of action research, it is not obvious whether traditional ideas about validity are comprehensive enough, since we are concerned, additionally, with the quality of relationships and the effectiveness of change.

Ideas about validity were originally designed to evaluate fixed designs using quantitative data, that is designs which are set before the main data collection phase begins. There is a considerable debate about their appropriateness for flexible or evolving designs, such as case study designs, using mainly or wholly qualitative data. The picture is somewhat further complicated by the fact that flexible designs may use some quantitative data and incorporate fixed designs within them. Indeed, we have been arguing that in many cases a mixed quantitative/qualitative approach is superior. In the following sections we discuss validity issues associated with fixed designs and then consider validity in the context of flexible designs. Practitioner researchers need to be aware of the range of validity issues in order to assess which are most appropriate for their own projects.

Validity and fixed designs

Validity in fixed designs is concerned with eliminating error and/or bias in measuring. In order to achieve a valid design, we need to be clear about the purpose of the research, the definitions of variables, the assumptions we make (especially about causality), and that any conclusions we draw are warranted.

We develop these points by considering a hypothetical example. An extra-curricular programme providing training for job interviews is offered to university students in their third year, with the intention of helping them to obtain graduate-level jobs. We wish to evaluate the success of this particular course in order to decide whether it should continue.

Before data collection begins certain decisions must be taken that could influence the credibility or validity of the research. For example we would need to decide how 'graduate-level jobs' are to be defined. They might be jobs that offer in-house training leading to professional qualifications, or those offering a certain salary level after two years' job experience, or they might be defined in terms of skill. If the definition is unpersuasive, then so will be the research.

Similar care has to be taken with the methods that use the definitions. If we want to decide whether to continue with the course we need to compare the participating students' job outcomes with those of the students who did not take the course. This necessitates collecting information about jobs, from both groups,

Table 8.1 Impact of a hypothetical training programme on job success

	Got a graduate-level job	Did not get a graduate-level job	Row total
Number of students who took the training programme	18	11	29
Number of students who did not take the training programme	7	19	26
Column total	25	30	55

most probably by graduates returning questionnaires (a poor response rate creates a major problem; however, for present purposes we will put this difficulty to one side).

We suppose that we have collected questionnaires from our sample of 55 graduates. Twenty-nine took the training course and twenty-six did not. Thirty of the sample did not obtain graduate-level jobs. How do we interpret these data? The simplest way is to recognise that there are four categories of student in our sample, and to record our numbers in a two-by-two classification table (see Table 8.1). In the top left cell of the table is the number of students who both obtained graduate-level jobs and took the training programme (18). In the cell below we have the number of students who have a graduate-level job without taking the training programme (7).

If the training programme made no difference (the null hypothesis) the chances of a student getting a graduate-level job would be similar whether or not they took the programme. The chances that a student who took the programme would get a graduate-level job, is the number that did both (18) compared with the total number who took the programme (29). The chance that a student who did not take the programme would get a graduate-level job is the smaller proportion, 7/26. At first sight, then, the programme is advantageous.

Is this difference significant ? Could it have come about purely by chance when the programme was actually ineffective? A chi-square statistic summarises how likely it is that the distribution between the four cells could have come about randomly. (How this is calculated is explained in any introductory statistics book, such as Ross 2005, or Denscombe 1998). There is apparently less than a one in a hundred chance that these particular results could have been obtained if the programme was ineffective – but see below.)

Causality (or internal validity)

We might assume that the positive association between those who took the course and gained a 'graduate-level job' means that the training programme was a significant factor in job success. However, it might be that the success of the programme for some students was due to extraneous factors. For instance the students who took the course might also have been exceptionally well connected through relatives and friends with people who could give them jobs.

Alternatively, if the table of numbers for the programme did not appear to show any significant difference in job placements according to whether or not graduates took the course, this may not mean that the course was ineffective. Suppose for instance we had two types of graduates, arts and engineering, and suppose also that engineering graduates normally had greater employability chances than arts graduates. If the engineering graduates did not attend the training, and the arts graduates did, we would not know about the effectiveness of the programme unless we controlled for graduates' type of degree.

The recommended solution for eliminating error or bias as much as possible is to design with specific threats to validity in mind. Robson (2002), following Cook and Campbell (1979), lists twelve possible types of threats to validity (see Robson 2002: 105, for a useful summary of different kinds of threat). We have already indicated one type, i.e. differences in the participants' characteristics that are not considered by the study, but which may have had an effect, and which could have been anticipated. The extraneous factors of job-related personal networks could have been taken into account as they are well documented in the literature on career choice. Similarly there are widely available data on differential graduate salaries by academic subject specialism.

Generalisability

What can we do with the results of our hypothetical study? This very much depends on our purposes. As presented here, it is small scale research, not controlling for extraneous influences. If we just want to decide whether to continue with the programme next year, we might assume that many of the extraneous factors will still be in place. If we are satisfied that we have understood their influences on the evaluation then the findings of Table 8.1 could be taken to support the decision to continue the course in this institution. On the other hand, it could be rash to extrapolate the findings to different environments. It may be simply that our results were very dependent on a particular lecturer and replicating the study at a different institution might generate different results. Even in the original institution, next year's outcomes may be very different, if for instance the labour market has collapsed as the economy has swung into recession.

Experiments

So far we have been recommending that practitioner researchers use multi-method case study approaches, possibly with some elements of fixed design and quantitative data where appropriate. Many lecturers with a scientific background may find this an uncongenial approach and wish to consider experimental designs, and indeed if we are considering an evaluative case study, it may be felt that an experiment is called for. In ordinary language we talk of experiments as being any sort of change we bring about when we try out something new: we may for example experiment with new cooking recipes, a new hair style or a new washing powder. If the changes seem positive, we are satisfied.

The 'experiment' in fixed design research has a much more precise meaning. A strict experiment involves assigning people or things to different conditions, and the manipulation of aspects or people, things, or conditions, that can be varied ('variables'). These aspects or properties can be measured and compared. Consider an example from botany of a strict experiment. Which of two fertilisers gives the better yield? Two fields are composed of the same soil, weather conditions and seed type (independent variables), the experimenter allocates different fertilisers to each (the 'experimental' or independent variable). The aim of the experiment is to see which fertiliser gives the best yield (the dependent variable) in these controlled conditions. If fertiliser type A turns out to be superior to type B, we are justified in telling a causal story. Seed type A outperforms seed type B, assuming a certain soil type, seed, certain set of weather conditions, and this particular fertiliser, i.e. all things being equal.

If we continue the hypothetical example of the interview training course, the variables might be age, gender, nationality, career-orientation, examination results: all can be measured. The term 'dependent variable' denotes the thing to be explained (i.e. as being dependent on the above independent variables); in our current example it is 'graduate-job success'. Those aspects or properties of things or people which can be changed by the manipulation are the independent variables.

Classrooms of students have been seen by some researchers, metaphorically, as 'fields', and experimental teaching methods or programmes as 'fertilisers' with the 'yield' measured in terms of examination results or some other outcome measure. Such randomised controlled trials (RCTs) are thought by many to be the best possible research design, a 'gold standard', especially in the USA (Oancea and Pring 2008). RCTs have been successful in medical research, but less successful in other contexts. Reasons for the failure of social RCTs have included the difficulty of controlling all the variables; for instance students may be absent, and unlike seeds, cannot be isolated from external influences. Nevertheless RCTs are as near as one may get to the strict experiment as understood by the physical scientist.

Experimental research has been criticised mainly on ethical grounds. These are discussed in Chapter 9. Here we note other drawbacks. Strict experiments presuppose a well worked out theory in advance of the research, normally generated by pre-existing theories, although this has been questioned by Popper (1963). In educational settings, convincing and well founded theories are often unavailable. Furthermore, educational settings are very complex, making it difficult to control all significant independent variables, as the discussion of the interview training course makes clear. There is also the problem that participants in an 'experiment' will exhibit the 'Hawthorne effect', that is they will alter their behaviour in an atypical fashion because they are being given special attention. Furthermore, strict experimentation involves random allocation of participants to experimental conditions. This assumes that one can construct groups that are equivalent:

failure to do so introduces the possibility that any change is due to differences in the group rather than the 'treatment'.

Quasi-experiments

In practitioner research, it is not usually practicable (or ethical) to use randomised groups. The quasi-experiment has been suggested as a solution. It involves an experimental approach using a single group or comparison groups, selected on some basis other than randomisation.

The job interview example was a quasi-experiment invoving comparison groups: the group that did take the course and the group that did not take the course. In that example we discussed specific threats to validity.

The single group quasi-experimental design needs particularly careful assessment of 'threats to validity'. The 'single group intervention post-test only' design does not *by itself* indicate that any improvement or deterioration was due to the intervention. An elementary principle for understanding the effects of an intervention is the creation of base-line data or evidence (such as examination scores of the group) before the intervention starts. Without this base-line we cannot usually convince others that the state of affairs (say, examination scores) after the intervention (post-test) was a consequence of the intervention. Yet this approach to innovation in education is quite common (see for example Stewart 1996).

More defensible is the 'single group pre-test intervention post-test' quasi-experimental design. We might consider the number of job interviews achieved by a group of third year undergraduates in their first term. Then suppose a course of CV writing and job targeting was introduced at the end of the term. The quasi-experiment then attributes the change in the group's job interview success between the first and second terms to the course. As the earlier discussion pointed out, threats to validity here include that the economic environment may have changed between the two terms among many other considerations.

These designs by themselves provide evidence that is likely to provide weak warrants for knowledge claims unless supplemented by other methods, as part of a multimethod case study approach, so that a persuasive case can be made. Jennings (2002) used the pre-test, intervention, post-test design with her class, but supplemented it with other sources of data, to make a very persuasive case for an approach to teaching spelling to primary school children who were behind their age group in reading attainment.

Multimethod approach

As we have noted, one reason why we contend that quantitative research, by itself, is not thought to be as useful as a multimethod approach, is that it does not necessarily develop understanding about why an intervention worked or did not, nor does it generate in-depth understanding of a situation. To return to our previous interview training example, we may find that the course was effective, but have no insight into why it was effective. Statistical information may be useful if we need to make a decision about whether to repeat it, but if we wish to develop and improve it we need qualitative information. Given the complexity of educational situations, there is much to be said for a mixed quantitative and qualitative methods approach. Quantitative data may indicate the presence of a problem, such as absenteeism from lectures, or a high examination failure rate amongst certain categories of students. Qualitative methods, such as focus groups, student diaries and observation may suggest tentative explanatory theories. Alternatively an initial study that is qualitative and exploratory may unearth a hunch that can be investigated by a quantitative approach such as a survey. Bryman usefully lists possible combinations of qualitative and quantitative methods (Bryman 1992: 59–61).

Validity and flexible designs

It will be remembered, from Chapter 3, that flexible research designs develop as the research progresses. Such designs usually employ mainly qualitative research methods. We need therefore to consider what constitutes validity in qualitative research. As with fixed designs, researchers should be concerned with the trustworthiness of their findings and, we suggest, in addition, a concern with useful knowledge.

Validity concerns apply at several points. First, any description has to be accurate. For example, one of the present authors interviewed six course team members about what qualities in students their business administration degree course hoped to develop. One interviewee's responses were so much at variance with those of the other lecturers that a follow-up interview was requested. This revealed that the lecturer had only recently taken up his post, and was in fact talking about the business administration degree course he had taught on at another university.

Since qualitative research is concerned with participants' meaning and actions, it would be invalid for the researcher to impose his or her meanings on what participants are saying or doing. 'Researcher bias' occurs when the researcher brings her own assumptions and preconceptions to her perceptions and interpretations. It is recommended that an awareness of one's own values and preoccupations be undertaken, and if appropriate, declared. This involves a great deal of self-awareness and knowledge. Preconceptions and biases are not easily identified and abandoned. An extreme example would be the lecturer who refuses to question the efficacy of her favourite methods of teaching a topic. The exercises at the end of Chapter 3 were devised partly with the intention of exploring such preconceptions and biases. This threat can also be reduced by 'member checking', that is any interpretation of meaning is checked with the participants. Similarly, bias can be eliminated by checking for alternative interpretations or explanations.

Triangulation is a commonly used strategy for increasing confidence in the researcher's interpretation of qualitative research. The basic idea is that perspectives, theories, or accounts can be checked using multiple sources of data (see Cohen et al. 2007: 142–43; Miles and Huberman 1984: 234–35).

External validity, or generalisability, was touched upon in Chapter 6, where the problem of the applicability of research findings to practice and of the advisability of generalising from small scale practitioner research was discussed. Here it was argued that case study allows for the development of insight into what is likely to 'work' in a particular setting. Stenhouse argued that knowledge generated by case study takes a retrospective rather than predictive form. 'Retrospective generalisations are attempts to map the range of experience rather than to perceive within that range the operation of laws in the scientific sense' (Stenhouse 1978: 22). In our example, where a course aims to improve job success, the case study would ideally provide a persuasive case. Quantitative research indicating that the course was effective, and qualitative research, perhaps pointing to differences in students who were successful and those who were not, would be illuminating. The emphasis would be on understanding the ways in which students interpreted and interacted with the programme and the way in which they had been able to use it. The research would help lecturers anticipate likely problems. A real example where this is currently happening is in the field of group work assessment in higher education. A number of studies have indicated recurring problems with the validity of common assessment approaches to group work in higher education. A good example of a multimethod case study, by Parsons and Drew (1996), illustrating this point is discussed in Chapter 10. Their study confirms what is already known, and usefully extends our knowledge by suggesting and evaluating new strategies.

Validity in action research

We mentioned above that some action research theorists have found traditional accounts of validity incomplete, or unsatisfactory. Bradbury and Reason (2006), for instance, suggest that there should be a concern with the quality of the relationships between participants. They suggest that all participants should be free to be 'maximally' involved. There should also be a concern about whether the participants in the research actually changed their actions, and more controversially whether the action research was inclusive of a 'plurality of knowing' using song, dance and the theatre as a way of presenting research work for validation. They also suggest that new infrastructures at the macro level, which sustain changes, could also be seen to validate action research.

McNiff and Whitehead (2006) also propose additional validity criteria relevant to action research. They suggest that the research demonstrates that it has led 'you to develop new forms of practice and new learning' and 'your possible contributions to new practices and theory' (McNiff and Whitehead 2006: 161).

And validity in auto/biographical research

Case study can utilise life history accounts, and it seems obvious that traditional scientific validity checks, or historical methods, are inappropriate. What therefore makes a personal story trustworthy? Griffiths and Macleod (2008) argue that validity, in one sense, means that the story has to be relevant and meaningful. They see this form of validity in narrative forms that consist either of ordinary typical stories or of atypical stories. The former have to be representative of peoples' ordinary lives; the latter should be significant for the reframing of our understanding that they allow. In addition, they argue that researchers should present an auto/biography in such a way that 'judgements can be made about its truthfulness and validity' (Griffiths and Macleod 2008: 134). They argue that the researcher should make clear to readers how she has taken various aspects of narrative, such as, for instance, its truthfulness, accuracy or sincerity, its representativeness, and its potential for re-framing topics. An example of the narrative approach is given by Churchman and King (2009). In their study, the stories of two groups of lecturers, one group on casual temporary contracts and another group on permanent contracts, were 'collaged' into two representative vignettes, with the aim of exposing the different ways in which increased university managerialism was impacting on their professional identities.

Griffith and Macleod's suggestions raise a more general point; it is the responsibility of the researcher to guide the reader of the research report about which validity issues are taken to be the most appropriate for the research design being employed and how 'threats' to validity posed by it have been tackled. The following section takes a 'flexible' design, action research, and indicates where validity issues may emerge as thinking develops throughout the study.

A hypothetical example

A possible action research question could be 'How can I (as a lecturer in, say, social studies) help dyslexic students to read and understand the course materials?' An action research approach is appropriate since I wish to change an aspect of my practice that I judge to be inadequate for certain students, who regularly complain, in course evaluations, that the course textbooks and additional written materials are too difficult. Action research starts with researching the problem, examining one's values and preconceptions. Here I have made the assumption that students who cannot read the text books for the course must be 'dyslexic', since I believe that undergraduates *should* be able to read at this level! Furthermore I think the course textbooks and written materials are adequate, if a bit turgid. On the other hand I would like the students to do well and grades are disappointing.

The research must, on the face of it, involve understanding the problems that dyslexic students have with the course materials. The discussion below follows the action research steps which have been explained in Chapter 7.

Problem specification or reconnaissance

In considering the problems as we have specified them, we are faced with two possible threats to validity. First, 'dyslexia' is an umbrella term for a number of different problems with reading (just as graduate-level jobs can be defined in a number of different ways). So it is unlikely that any one intervention would be suitable for all 'dyslexics'. Second, some have argued that the term 'dyslexia' is confusing and possibly mistaken in that it suggests that the condition is more than a loose way of referring to a number of reading difficulties. Stating the problem to be researched would require a critical appreciation of the debates surrounding the use of the term 'dyslexic' and a reasoned statement about how the term is being understood in the present research (see Chapter 5 for a discussion).

Ethical issues raise another possible threat to validity. Data on students with learning disabilities in higher education are confidential, and students may be reluctant to admit to being dyslexic. It may not be possible to research with students who have been identified as dyslexic (according to standard assessments), and it is questionable whether one should ask students to identify themselves, even if confidentiality is assured. It may only be possible to research with students who are willing to report some difficulty with reading materials (rather than admit to a learning disability). These students may include those without a dyslexia assessment. A possible threat to validity, then, is that the sample will be 'contaminated'.

Action research is a collaborative or cooperative form of research, and data are mainly collected and shared in class; therefore any approach that involves students 'admitting' a problem may cause evasion and embarrassment. This presents another possible threat to validity (a threat to the quality of relationships), since only the confident student will openly participate.

It is less problematic to involve the whole class in formative exercises or tests which can serve as a way of identifying the ways in which the materials engender reading problems rather than identifying the students who have reading problems. The message is that it is the materials that are deficient, not the students. Data from this exercise can then be shared with the class in a focused discussion of the kinds of reading problems experienced and the class can be invited to be co-inquirers into the design of better materials.

Some other possible threats to validity need to be taken into account. It may be that the materials are too difficult for the educational attainment of some students, as opposed to students experiencing reading difficulty. This raises the problem of what exactly is meant by 'reading' and 'reading difficulty' (see Chapter 5), a point that should be clarified and will require delving into the relevant literature.

Other factors leading to difficulties with written materials other than reading should be considered, as they may be relevant – for instance, lack of time. Some students may report pressure on time due to other responsibilities, such as child care. This helps to focus on what is a potential problem with the materials and what is largely outside the tutor's control. At this point a decision needs to be made about amending the original research question.

It may be more productive to ask 'What sorts of reading difficulties do my students experience with these particular materials? How can they be understood?

Are there any amendments to the written materials that could usefully be made to improve their learning and attainment?'

The ethics of practitioner research, as the brief discussion above indicates, are complex and are more fully discussed in Chapter 9. We recommended in Chapter 7 that any action research project should use a group of critical friends in an advisory capacity. Such a group should help one keep one's moral 'bearings' and provide some expertise. It would seem appropriate for this particular study to enlist the help of a lecturer specialising in literacy or dyslexia.

The intervention

Assuming the students have given fully informed consent for the research to go ahead and, if necessary, permission has been granted by your research ethics committee, and the students have agreed to be co-inquirers, the next stage of the inquiry is the implementation. The intervention(s) planned will arise in discussion with the students, the project's critical friends, and will be informed by theory derived from the literature searches carried out.

Among the possible threats to validity are: inability to judge whether the intervention had led to any improvement due to the intervention (and not to other factors); lack of comparative data (i.e. pre-intervention data); poor monitoring and execution of intervention; and lack of data on the outcome of the implementation.

Evaluating success or otherwise

Assuming the intervention went ahead as planned and data successfully collected, one should be in a position to make a judgement about the success or otherwise of the intervention. A possible threat to validity here is claiming more than the data will bear. It could be that the research question needs refining and the action research cycle needs to be started again.

Conclusion

The discussion of two hypothetical examples, one fixed (job interview training course) and the dyslexia study, which is flexible, demonstrate that validity takes many forms. It is integral to good research design, and failure to take it into account can seriously undermine the credibility and value of a research project.

Exercises

1   Imagine that you wish to evaluate the success of a new teaching method or set of materials. Discuss the approach you might take and any major threats to validity you may encounter.
2   Evaluate a research report in the area you wish to research. How has it conceptualised the problem of validity?

References

Bassey, M. (1999) *Case Study Research in Educational Settings.* Buckingham: Open University Press.

Bradbury, H. and Reason, P. (2006) 'Broadening the Bandwidth of Validity: Issues and Choice-points for Improving the Quality of Action Research', in P. Reason and H. Bradbury (eds) *A Handbook of Action Research.* London: Sage.

Bryman, A. (1992) 'Quantitative and Qualitative Research: Further Reflections on Their Integration', in J. Brannen (ed.) *Mixing Methods: Qualitative and Quantitative Research.* Aldershot: Avebury.

Churchman, D. and King, S. (2009) 'Academic Practice in Transition: Hidden Stories of Academic Identities', *Teaching in Higher Education* 14, 5: 507–16.

Cohen, L., Manion, L. and Morrison, K. (2007) *Research Methods in Education.* London: Routledge.

Cook, T. D. and Campbell, D. T. (1979). *Quasi-experimentation: Design and Analysis Issues for Field Settings.* Boston, MA: Houghton Mifflin.

Denscombe, M. (1998) *The Good Research Guide for Small-Scale Scale Social Reseach Projects.* Buckingham: Open University Press.

Foreman-Peck, L. and Murray, J. (2008) 'Action Research and Policy'. *Journal of the Philosophy of Education* 42, S1: 145–63.

Griffiths, M. and Macleod, G. (2008) 'Personal Narratives and Policy: Never the Twain?' *Journal of the Philosophy of Education* 42, S1: 121–43.

Jennings, S. (2002) 'Helping Weak Readers Up the Reading Ladder', in O. McNamara (ed.) *Becoming an Evidence-Based Practitioner: A Framework for Teacher-Researchers,* London and New York: RoutledgeFalmer.

McNiff, J. and Whitehead, J. (2006) *All You Need to Know about Action Research.* London: Sage.

Miles, M. B. and Huberman, A. M. (1984) *Qualitative Data Analysis: A Sourcebook of New Methods.* London: Sage.

Oancea, A. and Pring, R. (2008) 'The Importance of Being Thorough: On Systematic Accumulations of "What Works" in Education Research'. *Journal of the Philosophy of Education* 42, S1: 15–39.

Parsons, D. and Drew, S. (1996) 'Designing Group Project Work to Enhance Learning: Key Elements'. *Teaching in Higher Education* 1, 1: 65–80.

Popper, K. R. (1963) *Conjectures and Refutations: The Growth of Scientific Knowledge.* London: Routledge and Kegan Paul.

Robson, C. (2002) *Real World Research: A Resource for Social Scientists and Practitioner-Researchers.* Oxford: Blackwell.

Ross, S. M. (2005) *Introductory Statistics.* 2nd edn. Maryland Heights, MO: Academic Press.

Stenhouse, L. (1978) 'Case Study and Case Records: Towards a Contemporary History of Education'. *British Educational Research Journal* 4, 2: 21–39.

Stewart, M. (1996) 'Reflections on Teaching Physics to Science and Engineering Foundation Students'. *Teaching in Higher Education* 1, 2: 245–52.

Chapter 9

Researching responsibly
The ethics of practitioner research

Introduction

Ethics is concerned with morally right ways of acting, with the promotion of benefit and the avoidance of harm to the individuals with whom one has dealings. Whenever we have dealings with other people, ethical considerations are in play. Since research into one's own practice involves working with other people, ethical considerations are unavoidable. This chapter takes you through the main issues that you need to be concerned about, shows some of the pitfalls involved in not taking ethical issues seriously, and ends by discussing the usefulness, as well as the limitations of research ethics guidelines.

Initially, taking account of and responding to ethical constraints on one's research can seem like a daunting challenge. Can your students ever be suitable subjects for research, even as collaborators, when one's primary purpose as a lecturer is to benefit them? The benevolence of the lecturer, the imperative to do the best for his or her students, must surely be the overriding consideration. And, if that is so, what room is there for the possibility of using, or collaborating with one's students as subjects for one's research?

While benevolence is central to the teacher–student relationship, this does not mean that lecturers cannot do *anything* to improve their students' learning. We need to distinguish between the *ethical* constraint of benevolence and the *epistemic* one of a lack of knowledge as to the most effective ways of teaching and learning. And, on the latter subject, nearly every lecturer will admit at least a degree of uncertainty as to the most effective methods that could be employed, and therefore, to the duty (again suggested by the requirement of benevolence) to improve, wherever possible, the learning of his/her students.

Risk

One cannot, of course, *know* with any certainty whether teaching method X is better than teaching method Y, unless one has tried both extensively under comparable conditions. This does not mean to say that *any* X is plausibly likely to be better than *any* Y. We do, very often, have very good reasons to suppose that doing X rather than Y is likely to do more harm than good based on personal experiences, professional wisdom or research evidence. Reflection on one's personal and professional experience, together with knowledge of extant research should, therefore, eliminate many possible but obviously outlandish alternatives to established practice, even as plausible avenues for exploration.

It is a sad testimony to the care taken by some educational researchers that such precautions are sometimes not taken before new methods are tried. A notorious example is the 'real books' approach to teaching reading, which was influential for some years in UK primary schools (Waterland 1985).

A first ethical constraint, therefore, in pedagogical research, is the need to minimise the risk of harm due to the introduction of an innovation. This is related to a more general point that is sometimes overlooked by innovators. In considering an innovation one needs to consider the balance of advantages and disadvantages that may result. The balance sheet of innovation does not always lie on the advantage side of the ledger, and one needs to be confident that the advantages outweigh the disadvantages. That said, one's benevolence will also very often suggest a duty to improve one's practice whenever one has good reason to suppose that a change of pedagogic method is likely to bring about such a result. The need to innovate is as much driven by benevolence as is the need for caution in innovation. The apparent dilemma is largely avoided by 'due diligence' when considering possible means of securing pedagogic improvement. A great part of any such due diligence is, therefore, careful reflection on what is already known, both in the research literature and in one's own personal pedagogic experience and, particularly in the case of younger professionals, in the experience of their more senior colleagues.

Innovation and research design

Benevolence thus seems to recommend a cautious but positive approach to innovation. The practitioner researcher must have good reason to suppose that the innovation will benefit students with virtually no risk of serious harm coming to them, either in their ability to learn or in any other way. What does such an approach mandate as research designs within this twofold constraint of benevolence – the need to innovate and the need to be cautious? The first point that comes to mind is the need to do something. After all, if one has good reasons to suppose that method X, which one is currently employing, is less than optimally effective, and if, further, one has good reasons to suspect that method Y is more effective than X, one has a prima facie duty to introduce Y, subject of course to an evaluation of the relative effectiveness of methods X and Y.

This seems to suggest that the lecturer is only entitled to use studies in which an intervention is introduced to the whole cohort. Further reflection, however, suggests slightly more flexibility than this. One may collect data with a previous cohort, anticipating a future need for an intervention and then, with a subsequent cohort, introduce an intervention. In effect, this gives one a time-lagged quasi-experimental design. What does seem to be excluded is a quasi-experimental study in which part of the cohort receives the preferred pedagogic intervention and the other does not. If one has good reason to believe that method Y is better than method X and one is trying to be benevolent to all one's students, one can hardly use X on one part of the group and Y on another, without violating this constraint.

There is, apparently, no easy answer to this question. Time-lagged quasi-experiments and designs without a control group seem to impose very severe constraints on the permissible design possibilities for lecturers contemplating intervention and innovation in their pedagogic methods. Nevertheless, there are possibilities worth considering. In the introduction of an innovation for research purposes, even where the primary purpose of the intervention is pedagogic, it is desirable to obtain *informed consent* from the subjects of one's intervention. If students understand the 'downside risk' and if it is not too great, then it may be possible to conduct a controlled intervention study or even a randomised control trial (RCT). On the other hand, if it becomes sufficiently evident that either the intervention or the control group believe that they are benefitting less than the other group, it needs to be understood that students should be allowed to migrate to the pedagogy that is being seen to provide the most benefit. Not to allow this to happen is to violate the stance of benevolence that is one of the cardinal occupational virtues of the teacher. A good example is the West Dunbartonshire Literacy Initiative (MacKay 2006), a quasi-experimental study in a small Scottish local education authority which had the avowed aim of eliminating illiteracy amongst the school population over a ten-year period (1997–2007). It is obvious that the aim of this study was to benefit the schoolchildren and their community. The intervention group received a structured programme of some six complementary elements in the teaching of reading which, it was believed, after a background literature review by the researchers, had strong evidence of effectiveness. At an early stage in the project the beneficial effects of the intervention programme became obvious to the teachers in the control group schools. As a result, they all wished to move to the interventions being implemented in the experimental group schools. The research team accepted this as they could hardly (and did not wish to) deny children in the control group schools what seemed to their teachers and to the researchers to be the self-evident benefits of the intervention. As Mackay explains, this is one of the 'hazards' of being involved in implementing complex research designs where people's lives and interests are involved. One cannot rigidly stick to research designs which deny some of the subjects self-evident benefits.

It can be argued that the initial adoption of a quasi-experimental design in this case was justified by the possible downside risk of using a study that only incorporated an intervention for all the schools and which thus was unable to assess the relative efficacy of the intervention as opposed to non-intervention. After all, there may be unforeseen consequences in the adoption of relatively unknown techniques in a complex environment in which they had not been tried before.

Particularly at the early stages of any such research programme, it would be justifiable to ensure that such possible risks were at least assessed as early as possible. By comparing a control with an intervention group, the nature of such risks would become clearer and modifications to the intervention more easily made. But such an approach cannot be sustained if the risks do not become apparent and the advantages of the intervention make themselves manifest.

We conclude, therefore, that while the imperative of benevolence does mandate a variety of research designs, they are all beholden to the imperative, and the researcher must be prepared to adapt if circumstances change, as in the example above. Just as the duty of benevolence has a fairly obvious resonance with anyone with a basic moral sensibility, so do most of the other common ethical pitfalls that researchers need to avoid. There is no specialist moral knowledge and there are no moral experts, although expertise may sometimes be required in order to guide a subject through the ethically sensitive aspects of a complex situation. The fact that these constraints are often ignored is largely down to common moral failings on the part of researchers, such as insensitivity, over-eagerness to satisfy curiosity, and the desire for fame.

Some ethical pitfalls in research design and execution

The research literature is full of examples of where ethical constraints on research have either been neglected or completely ignored. Although these mistakes may seem obvious when pointed out, they were not always so obvious when they were committed for the reasons just mentioned above. It is, therefore, instructive to look at some of these. But one point should be noted. We have argued that practitioner-based research must take account of the fact that the primary purpose of the activity which is being researched and for which the practitioner is responsible is the successful learning of the students who are his or her responsibility. Non-practitioner researchers do not have this responsibility, but they are nevertheless subject to ethical constraints through the possibility of good or harm that they may do to their subjects by researching them. There follow some examples from the literature of the kinds of mistakes that have been made by researchers over the years.

Project Camelot was a study commissioned by the US government but never actually put into effect, which aimed to study the causes of revolutions with the intention of finding ways of preventing them (Smith 1975). It was assumed that revolutions were necessarily a bad thing, to be prevented if possible. In this case, the ethical assumptions that lay behind the study were questionable, since it may be doubted whether revolutions are always a bad thing, particularly when they are directed against brutal and corrupt regimes. The researchers in Project Camelot were making an implicit normative judgement about certain kinds of political event which is, to say the least, morally contestable. They appeared to assume that all revolutions are harmful, irrespective of the nature of the regime against which they are directed.

A study in Tuskegee, Alabama, in 1932 looked at the effects on a group of black men suffering from syphilis in order to learn about the progression of the disease (Smith 1975). No medical help was offered to the sufferers. In this case, although the primary purpose of the study was medical research, it blatantly failed the test of benevolence since the aims of the designers of the study, to under- stand the progression of syphilis, took precedence over the welfare of the sub- jects. Not only is there a failure of benevolence evident in this study, but there was a wilful lack of concern for the welfare of the subjects of the study, that is, a neglect of the duty to protect them from harm. There are other egregious examples of disregard of the welfare of subjects. Milgram's (1963) study on obedience deceived subjects into thinking that they were inflicting painful electric shocks on victims who failed to answer questions correctly. The subjects were distressed or ran the risk of being distressed through their awareness that they had apparently inflicted considerable suffering on their 'victims'. Deliberate deception was also used in that the subjects were not told the purpose of the experiment, which was to measure propensity to obedience, and they were also made to believe that they were inflicting suffering when in fact they were not doing so – the writhing victims were in fact writhing actors. It is clear that in this case there was a lack of concern for the welfare of the subjects of the research, deception, and a failure to secure informed consent.

Another study that did not rely on deception but which did appear to be cavalier with the well-being of the subjects was Zimbardo's (1972) study of a simulated prison in which subjects were asked to act the role of either prison guards or prisoners. It quickly became clear that the 'prison guards' entered their roles with considerable gusto and dealt out pretty robust treatment to the 'prisoners', who suffered as a result. Harm was therefore done to both groups of subjects, to the 'prisoners' because of the rough treatment that they received and also to the 'guards' when they had a later opportunity to reflect on their behaviour during the course of the experiment. The Milgram and Zimbardo studies are also good examples of manipulative behaviour, where there is a lack of due regard for the feelings and welfare of the subjects and they are put into humiliating or com- promising positions for the sake of the research. One might say of the Zimbardo study that, even when informed consent had been given, it was not in the sub- jects' powers to properly give informed consent since they could not adequately foresee the consequences of their agreeing to take part in the experiment.

Another kind of doubtful case to be found in the research literature is where observation without the subjects' consent takes place. Humphrey's (1970) covert study of homosexual soliciting in public toilets falls into this category. This study is also notorious for its use of deception to gain access for interviews and viola- tion of privacy by tracking subjects to their homes using licence plate numbers. A less controversial example is the use of 'the mystery shopper' in consumer sur- veys. Subject awareness is also a major issue in sociolinguistic studies where it is important to obtain natural speech samples. Labov (1969) and Tizard and Hughes (1984) provide ingenious examples of how this can be done without violating the interests or the right to consent of the subjects. Labov achieves this by overtly introducing the researcher into the group to be researched and allowing the group to become accustomed to his presence. Tizard and Hughes recorded interactions between nursery teachers and children using randomly activated radio microphones. The subjects (and their parents) knew they were being recorded but did not know exactly when. These examples indicate that careful reflection about research design factors can often resolve ethical issues that arise from the research problem.

Other factors that need to be carefully taken into account are confidentiality and property rights. There are often very good reasons why it would not be in the subject's interests to be identified. This is as true of institutions as much as it is of individuals. Even when the researcher does not consider that publicity will damage the interests of subjects it is still important that subjects' own wishes for privacy and confidentiality are respected. The researcher will have to give careful consideration as to whether confidentiality may be breached, where, for example, the population from which a sample is drawn is very small and each individual member has distinctive characteristics. Particular kinds of design may lead to problems. For example, longitudinal studies may lead to a situation where consent needs to be obtained during the study (e.g. a child coming of age). Property rights to data that accrue over long periods of study also need to be respected.

Thinking systematically about practitioner research ethics

It should be apparent that researching responsibly requires careful ethical deliberation. In the sections following, we will set out how to think about ethical issues in an organised way through the discussion of examples, and suggest practical advice where possible. We can think about ethical issues as occurring at three stages of research: the planning stage, the implementation stage, and the writing up or reporting stage.

The planning stage

Various professional associations, such as the British Sociological Association, have produced guidance for the ethical conduct of research in their disciplines. In the field of education, the British Educational Research Association's *Ethical Guidelines* (BERA 2004) are widely used by educational researchers, and the ESRC's research ethics framework is also a useful source of guidance for social scientists (ESRC 2005). The BERA guidelines set out the principles and responsibilities that, the Association believes, ought to be binding for their members and are recommended for non-members engaged in educational research. They also set out researchers' obligations which must be met in respect of legislation such as the Data Protection Act (1998). The BERA guidelines are organised under three main headings: responsibilities to participants, to sponsors of research (if any), and to the community of educational researchers. We recommend that all three sections should be read by practitioner researchers; the first section, however, is of most relevance to teachers researching their own practice

It should also be remembered that universities normally have policies and procedures governing the conduct of research by lecturers, and these should be followed: indeed they are required by any university holding an ESRC grant. University or college faculties or departments may also have their own procedures for reviewing and approving research projects. These may offer more detailed and specific advice or requirements, such as how to anonymise video recordings, or how to store data securely.

In respect of the planning stage of research, the BERA guidelines suggest that the following steps are taken: securing the fully informed voluntary consent of participants; giving the right to participants to withdraw at any stage; gaining permission from relevant people or authorities where necessary (for example where children or vulnerable adults are involved); and giving information to participants about how their interests will be protected. The ethic of respect for persons, which is one of the principles in the BERA guidelines, requires that all participants in the research, as has been said, voluntarily give their fully informed consent. The notion of a participant includes collaborators, colleagues, or others, whether they are actively engaged or just passively part of the context (BERA 2004: 4). In thinking through these actions, we recommend that you ask yourself the following questions, so that you are clear in your own mind about your ethical approach, before any field work or implementation takes place.

1 What is the research about (purpose, methods, and intended possible uses)?
2 Who are the participants (active, engaged or part of the context)? Why is the participant's involvement necessary? What does their participation entail and what are the risks to them, if any? Are any vulnerable adults involved, or children under 18?
3 Will others have access to the data/evidence, beside the researcher(s)?
4 How will confidentiality of information be maintained?
5 How will the data be stored securely and when will it be disposed of?
6 How will the anonymity of participants be assured? (If anonymity is not possible and participants are named in any report or are identifiable in any other way, what measures will be taken to ensure that they are not harmed?)
7 What actions will you take if you meet an unanticipated ethical problem once the research is under way?

These matters should be thought through as part of the ethical approach of the research. Some need to be clarified in order to convince participants that their interests will not be harmed. Your university will also have an interest in seeing that the research will not bring it into disrepute.

Although the principles in the BERA guidelines are clearly stated, they only state what would be normally expected. Guidelines cannot take into account the particularities of situations, and what may be generally recommended as good practice may not seem to hold in particular cases, or for particular research designs. There are many 'grey' areas in research ethics, and even at the planning stage it can be difficult to decide what the right thing to do is. Deliberation is essential. The following example illustrates these points.

Philipot (1993) set up an action research inquiry in order to see whether the seating arrangements in his language classroom influenced his students' frequency of spoken contributions to the lesson. His hunch was that some seats allowed some students to 'hide' and others to dominate. He hypothesised that he could improve the interaction in his class by altering the seating arrangements. He considered that the research data could be collected without undue interference to his normal teaching, and this was true for his colleagues who agreed to research the same problem, but at different locations. Philipot's school was one of a chain of private language schools teaching English, in this case to students over the age of 16 years. Because he felt able to conduct the research without altering his normal teaching (although changing the seating arrangements and his own usual spatial location), and he was himself the head teacher, he felt that he did not need to seek the permission of the owner-managers of his school, nor of his colleagues or students to carry out the research.

As he himself realised, this decision breaches the ethical imperative to seek the 'voluntary informed consent' of those involved in the research. The BERA guidelines state that 'researchers must take the necessary steps to ensure that all participants in the research understand the processes in which they are engaged, including why their participation is necessary, how it will be used and to whom it will be reported', and action researchers 'must consider the extent to which their own reflective research impinges on others' (BERA 2004: 5). On the other hand, the guidelines also state that 'researchers must avoid deception or subterfuge *unless* their research design specifically requires it to ensure that the appropriate data is collected' (our italics, BERA 2004: 5). Where deception or subterfuge has been thought to be unavoidable, the guidelines recommend 'full deliberation and subsequent disclosure in reporting'. They recommend that approval be sought from a local or institutional ethics committee, and that if possible to do so, researchers seek consent on a 'post-hoc basis in cases where it was not desirable to seek it before undertaking the research'. (BERA 2004: 5). Thus it is not clear from the guidelines whether Philipot's failure to gain his students' fully informed consent is unethical or not.

Philipot explains: 'I was uneasy about this deception, but could not really see how it would be possible to tell them [i.e. the students] they were part of a research project without vitiating the internal validity of the study – since one of the basic points was that it was an observation of their normal spontaneous, seating patterns' (1993: 193). We may ask, was Philipot's approach ethically defensible?

The following discussion is a possible line of argument that others might wish to disagree with, as with any deliberation. We can start to think about the situation by first considering who is part of the context. In this case, we could argue that there are five categories of people who are involved. The school owner-managers senior to Philipot; the students in his and his researching colleagues' classes; the group of researching teachers; and other teachers working in the schools and other students in the school who are not participating in the research. Some categories are 'passive': the owner-managers are not actively engaged in the research as participants, nor are the non-researching teachers and their students; they are, however, part of the context, and there may or may not be adverse consequences for them or the research. The students in the researched classes are more directly affected, unknowingly, as subjects. Last, the researching teachers working in parallel with Philipot, are active, i.e fully engaged in the research. For each category of person we could ask what harm might accrue to them as a result of the research. Here we will concentrate on the two that are, on the face of it, most directly involved: the owner-managers and the researched students.

Arguments for and against Philipot's decision

It could be argued that qua teacher Philipot could have rearranged the seating in his class as part of his reflective teaching practice, and he would not have needed to ask anyone for permission. An obvious difference, however, is that research, unlike reflective practice, involves the systematic collection of data on students, which is a different activity, with different intentions from teaching. Students enter into a teaching situation on the understanding that they are to be taught, not used as research subjects. We might argue that an implicit contract between teacher and taught is being contravened.

But someone might say that, on the face of it, there is no obvious or foreseeable harm involved in what is proposed and that Philipot's intentions are praiseworthy. Against this we may point out that although we cannot foresee ethical problems at this point in time, it does not mean that there won't be any. There are many examples where good intentions have resulted in unforeseen perverse effects. Indeed, Philipot himself senses that there is an ethical problem, but thinks he has no alternative choice. And indeed we may concede that deceiving people is usually wrong, but not always. In exceptional cases, we may feel that we have no choice, if the consequences of not deceiving someone are catastrophic; for instance, we might lie to a murderer to save the life of a potential victim; but Philipot's case is not like this. What is at stake is a concern with 'internal validity'. This is hardly a life or death matter.

Nevertheless, someone might still insist that Philipot's deception is justified because it really is impossible to imagine how anyone could possibly be harmed, and if useful knowledge is gained for the benefit of others, then his deception is justified. So in what could harm consist? It could be argued that there *is* a likely detriment which applies to all acts of deception: a corrosion of trust. Teachers should be moral exemplars. Once students found out about the deception, and the breaking of their implicit understanding, their trust in him as a teacher – possibly in all teachers – and in their institution might be compromised, to the detriment of the teacher–student relationship. Thus we might argue that deception is not justified.

Let us now turn to the other participants who are part of the context, the owner-managers. In their case, we could argue that they have a right to know, since research (like all research on or with people), has the potential to produce unintended harm, and here what could be harmed is the school's reputation, as well as the well being of the students. Where the risk seems minimal, as in Philipot's study, it could still be argued that as a matter of prudence and courtesy, the owner managers still ought to be informed, since they might face some embarrassment if there are subsequently unanticipated problems and questions are asked about it in public, or by parents. The risk, of course, is that the owner-managers might object to the research and prevent a possibly innovative and improved approach to teaching being developed, albeit one involving deception. The risk seems slight, however, as the intervention seems innocuous and has potential benefits in terms of student learning.

Part of the initial confusion about the ethical wisdom of Philipot's approach was a lack of appreciation of an alternative that did not compromise 'internal validity'. Some observations may be pertinent to our deliberations here. It certainly is not in the spirit of action research to use deception (see Chapter 7). We have already noted that action research involves participants in the research as having a say in problem definition. Philipot does not share his perception of a problem with the interaction in the class, with his students, for the reasons stated above. Action researchers research *with*, rather than *on* participants for moral and epistemological reasons, so we may question at the outset whether he has adopted an appropriate model of research. Philipot's research design is more like an experiment: but even experimental research requires informed consent.

Possible solutions

In Philipot's case a better ethical strategy would involve 'coming clean' about the research with students and staff, asking that students act naturally regarding their seating preferences, and acknowledge the fact in reporting the research that once alerted, the students' choices may have been influenced. The extent to which they felt self-conscious about their seating choices could be determined by other methods, such as a questionnaire. Some may feel that this strategy weakens any claims made. But, we could argue, it is a price worth paying to maintain good teacher–student relationships. Alternatively, Philipot could have outlined his research in general terms, with reassurances that they, the students, would not be harmed by it and then disclosed more fully the nature of the research after its completion. Yet another alternative would have been to describe the proposed research in detail, but not reveal the stage at which it would be carried out. This latter strategy overcomes any tendency the students may have to act 'unnaturally'.

The right to withdraw

Another complicating factor brought out by the Philipot case, and one that practitioner researchers face more generally, is that in seeking their students' informed consent they may feel unduly pressured. Lecturers are also assessors, and students may not wish to forfeit their teacher's positive regard. As Homan puts it, 'students may be rendered powerless to refuse' (Homan 2001: 331). Are Philipot's students in a position to refuse to take part? What would *not* taking part consist of? Presumably students who did not want to be studied would not be listed on the diagrams that he made of students' seating choices after each teaching session, but they would have to experience him altering his own physical location in the classroom. Furthermore, if only one student withdrew, he or she would still be identifiable by the gap in the data. Assurances of confidentiality might overcome this difficulty, but it seems that the possibility of withdrawing from the intervention altogether (i.e. Philipot's changing his position) is not available. It seems that students who do not wish to be researched can only partly withdraw, and it would be up to Philipot to negotiate an acceptable arrangement with them. However, we would argue that the right to research one's teaching, in the sense of trying to improve methods, as opposed to the sense in which data is collected on individuals, and where there is no predictable harm to students, should override the right of students to veto any innovations.

The ethics of collaboration

An ethical approach to the conduct of collaborative relationships with researching colleagues is also important. The BERA guidelines are explicit about authorship claims (see BERA 2004: 12), but are silent about the conduct of collaborative relationships and the principles that should inform them. It seems sensible that individual responsibilities for data collection, storage and disposal, analysis and writing up should be agreed at the start, along with the number and pattern of meetings to discuss progress, analyse data and deliberate.

Confidentiality and anonymity

Assurances of confidentiality and anonymity should also be carefully considered at the planning stage. Such promises are given to protect the identity of the participants. This is necessary to protect them from any harmful consequences of sensitive or negative findings, or indeed the stigmatisation of institutions or communities (see for example the case of Mary Chamberlin in Tickle 2001). Accidental breaches of confidentiality and anonymity are therefore serious and can have serious consequences. The requirements of the Data Protection Act (1998) should be adhered to (BERA 2004: 8; see also ESRC's ethical framework, ESRC 2005: 18–19). Careful thought should be given to the possibility that complete anonymity in reporting is impossible. In case study research, we have argued, the context and background features are important for other researchers or lecturers to be able to generalise findings to their own contexts. But this requirement may serve to identify participants. Backgrounds and contexts can be disguised to a certain extent. For example the gender, age, and location may be altered and pseudonyms used. But this has to be carefully done so as not to produce a distorted picture. It may be more prudent to admit that there is a potential for identification and instead to give participants the right to edit any account. A consequence of this is that some sensitive data or evidence may have to be left out.

The implementation and data collection stage

Getting one's ethical strategy clear at the planning stage can, as we have seen from the above example, require careful deliberation, but even where one is confident about one's ethical strategy, unanticipated ethical problems may arise during the conduct of the research, and these will also require deliberation. Perhaps the most common problem is the accidental discovery of wrongdoing or serious unprofessional behaviour. Decisions have to be made about whether to break assurances of confidentiality and anonymity one has given to participants, and reveal their identity to those in authority who have an obligation to act.

It is acknowledged in the BERA guidelines that the decision to deliberately break confidentiality and anonymity promises is a very serious matter. However, the guidance offered by BERA to researchers in this position is minimal. They recommend thorough deliberation, and the keeping of contemporaneous notes, in case of a misconduct complaint (BERA 2004: 8).

Although one is not morally responsible for the disclosed or witnessed wrongdoing, the discovery of it requires a decision about what to do. Keeping silent inevitably leads to feelings of guilt and may in fact be morally wrong, despite the confidentiality and anonymity promises given. The discovery of criminal behaviour or sexual abuse, for example, places a strong moral obligation on the researcher to either help the victim, who may have disclosed, or to report the agent who has disclosed. This is especially the case where the people involved are minors or vulnerable adults.

Some cases are not clear cut. For example, one of the present authors, while researching, witnessed a teacher, seemingly unprovoked, strike a pupil during a lesson. Having given assurances of confidentiality placed her in a difficult position. Was this incident of such a serious nature that confidentiality ought to have been broken? Was this a one-off incident or part of a persistent attack on this student? The incident occurred long before universities had established policies and procedures. Discussion with her tutor did not resolve the issue. In retrospect something should have been done, since it is possible that this teacher may have abused other children. We could say that the teacher demonstrated a lack of respect and benevolence towards this student, and should have been reported. In the end, however the matter was 'swept under the carpet'.

Campbell discusses a similar incident of an unprovoked attack on a pupil, although she was not researching at the time, and had therefore given no reassurances about confidentiality (Campbell 2001). She reported the incident to her principal, who refused to act, saying that the responsibility for confronting the wrongdoer lay with her. She writes, with regret, that at the time she lacked the 'moral courage' to intervene and was worried about her relationship with other staff if she were seen as a snitch (Campbell 2001: 403). These examples highlight the point that it is sometimes difficult to decide on the right course of action by oneself. Support for deliberation is needed, and most universities now have procedures in place for such incidents to be discussed by tutors and, if need be, by research ethics committees.

Incidents of unprofessional behaviour or professional wrongdoing are not, of course, confined to the school age population. Lecturers may accidentally discover unprofessional conduct by colleagues and instances of wrongdoing by students.

The writing up and reporting stage

Ethical problems at this stage of the research are usually concerned with maintaining promises of confidentiality and anonymity. To assure someone of confidentiality means that what has been said or witnessed will not be repeated, in an irresponsible way, to third parties. Closely tied to the idea of confidentiality therefore is the idea of protecting participants' interests in reporting findings. Thus assurances of anonymity are usually given and participants are given pseudonyms. Ethical issues arise when it becomes apparent that participants and institutions are likely to be identified. As we noted earlier, problems can be avoided by giving this matter some thought at the planning stage.

If it is likely that despite reassurances participants may be identified, it is best to admit it to them. It may be that participants do not mind being identified, in which case it is usual practice to obtain their written permission. But it is still incumbent on the researcher to ensure that their interests are safeguarded. In some cases, however, the participant will object, and that part of one's research will have to be sacrificed.

Exercises

1 Produce two short information sheets setting out details of your research project. One should be designed for students whom you wish to invite to take part and the other for lecturers and others who are part of the research context. Use BERA's 2004 *Ethical Guidelines*, and any specific guidance produced by your university or college, to help you decide what should be said.
2 Imagine that during your research incidents of wrongdoing have been disclosed (e.g. bullying, cheating, sexual intimidation). Find out what your university or colleges procedures are.
3 Imagine that you are going to work collaboratively on a research project with your colleagues. Analyse all the research tasks that need to be undertaken. Write an informal contract setting out who will be responsible for what and how issues of authorship will be decided.

References

British Educational Research Association (BERA) (2004) *Ethical Guidelines*. Available at www.bera.ac.uk/publications/pdfs/ethical.pdf.

Campbell, E. (2001) 'Let Right be Done: Trying to Put Ethical Standards into Practice'. *Journal of Educational Policy* 16, 5: 395–411.

ESRC (2005) *Ethical Framework for Social Scientists*. Available at www.esrc.ac.uk/esrcInfoCentre/index.aspx.

Homan, R. (2001) 'The Principle of Informed Consent: The Ethics of Gatekeeping'. *Journal of the Philosophy of Education* 35, 3: 329–43.

Humphreys, L. (1970) *Tearoom Trade: Impersonal Sex in Public Places*. London: Duckworth.

Kemmis, S. and McTaggart, R. (1981) *The Action Research Planner*. Geelong, VIC: Deakin University Press.

Labov, W. (1969) 'The Logic of Nonstandard English', in P.-P. Giglioli (ed.) (1972) *Language and Social Context* (pp. 179–215). London: Penguin.

MacKay, T. (2006) *The West Dunbartonshire Literacy Initiative*. West Dunbartonshire Council.

McNamee, M. (2001) 'The Guilt of Whistle-blowing: Conflicts in Action Research and Educational Ethnography'. *Journal of the Philosophy of Education* 35, 3: 423–41.

Milgram, S. (1963) 'A Behavioural Study of Obedience'. *Journal of Abnormal and Social Psychology* 67: 371–78.

Philipot, P. (1993) 'Seating Patterns in Small Language Classes: An Example of Action Research'. *British Educational Research Journal* 19, 2: 191–210.

Smith, F. (1985) *Reading*. Cambridge: Cambridge University Press.

Smith, H. W. (1975) *Strategies of Social Research*. Milton Keynes: Open University Press.

Tickle, L. (2001) 'Opening Windows, Closing Doors: Ethical Dilemmas in Educational Action Research'. *Journal of the Philosophy of Education* 35, 3: 345–59.

Tizard, B. and Hughes, M. (1984) *Young Children Learning*. London: Fontana.

Waterland, E. (1985) *Read With Me*. Stroud: Thimble Press.

Zimbardo, P. G. (1972) 'The Pathology of Imprisonment'. *Society* 6, 4: 6–8.

Chapter 10

Examples of practitioner research case studies

Introduction

In this chapter we review four published practitioner research case studies: an action research study, a quasi-experimental study, a grounded theory study, and an evaluation, all of which illustrate various ways in which empirical research can be used to inform the development of practice. All research has strengths and limitations, and the case studies presented here are not flawless. Nevertheless, they address teaching, learning and curriculum design problems of interest to lecturers in higher education, and offer evidence-informed practical strategies, insights, or further directions for investigation.

In offering a critical commentary on the case studies, we highlight important points about the value, design and conduct of practitioner research case studies. Each case study is introduced and its potential interest outlined. It is then discussed, drawing on the quality criteria for practitioner research suggested in Chapter 3, and the key elements of research design discussed in Chapter 7.

Case study 1

Parsons, D. E. and Drew, S. K. (1996) 'Designing Group Project Work to Enhance Learning: Key Elements'. Teaching in Higher Education 1, 1: 65–80

The authors' starting point is the dissatisfaction expressed by students about group work assignments. In the first year of their degree in housing studies, students have had considerable experience of group work. Despite its unpopularity, the authors nevertheless decided to introduce it into two second year modules, covering housing design and development. The rationale for doing this was that their employer's forum encouraged it, and they believed that group work could lead to a better learning experience, since multiple points of view could be shared. The authors believed that problems with group work identified by staff, students and the literature could be overcome by careful attention to task design. They intended to diagnose the problem, introduce a possible solution and evaluate its success. The design is similar, therefore, to a technical action research design, although the authors are not explicit about this and make no reference to the methodological literature.

The authors consulted the thirty students taking the modules and lecturers in their department with experience of teaching in this mode about their opinions of group work. The students' objections were summarised as: 'concern for their own individual grade; unequal contributions by group members affecting both work load and individual grades; logistical problems in meeting together and the resulting extra demands on their time' (p. 67). They expressed the view that these problems introduced unfairness in the assessment, hindered student motivation, and diverted attention from the subject matter and the development of skills. Tutors expressed concern about the possibility of fair assessment, unsatisfactory group composition and the allocation of tasks that allowed some students merely to practise skills already mastered (p. 69).

The authors chose to address some of these problems by focusing on the organisation of the group work task, and the balance between student choice and tutor direction in the assessment strategy. They provided written guidance for students in the form of briefing notes on group processes, the output required, the assessment arrangements, and an introduction to the design process. To overcome logistical problems in finding times and places to meet, the groups were assigned a three-hour block of time (presumably each week), for one semester, with a tutor on hand to help with any difficulties. The resources needed for the task were provided. The groups were randomly composed. To overcome the problem of absentee students, a sliding scale of penalties was introduced for unexplained absences. For example, if a student had three unexplained absences their work would be marked out of 90 per cent, four absences out of 80 per cent, and so on.

The problem with the assessment of the project was conceptualised as a lack of choice about how to be assessed. The hypothesised solution was to allow students to be assessed either as a group (with the same group mark for each member), or as an individual (a mark for the part of the task assigned to the individual student), or a mixture of group mark and individual marks. To overcome the possibility of those students opting for individual marks meeting solely to divide the task at the beginning and, for presentation purposes, at the end, the task was designed so that some parts could not be completed without group members consulting with each other.

Since the point of group working is the development of group working skills, the authors felt that there was a need to assess the process. Thus they asked the students to provide a critical evaluation of how the group worked, with evidence such as notes of meetings, and it was emphasised that a good mark did not depend on having established an effective group, but on a critical analysis and reflection on how things could have been improved.

The evaluation phase of the research focused on whether the design of the group work project had met some of the students' concerns. In a structured discussion students were asked how the present project differed from other group work projects they had experienced, what was good about it and how it could be improved. They were also asked how they had chosen to be assessed and how this had affected their group working. Finally they were given a questionnaire asking them how far they agreed with five statements.

The majority of students reported that the organisation of the present project had been better than previous ones. It differed in that a room and time was provided, there were penalties for non-attendance, and guidance and tutor support was provided. They made some recommendations for improved tutor support, such as regular feedback on progress and help with conflicts. On assessment, those who had opted to be marked individually did meet with the whole group minimally (as feared), but also met in sub-groups when necessary. These students liked this arrangement, partly because they were marked as individuals, partly because they could avoid inter-personal difficulties. Those groups that had decided on a group mark worked very co-operatively. The questionnaire confirmed that students appreciated having a choice over how to be assessed, and that they approved the penalising of non-attending students. They were, however, less appreciative of group working as an experience. The final comments made on the questionnaire all referred to unhappiness with group working, even though they thought that this project had been well managed.

Therefore the authors hypothesise that getting the conditions and assessment arrangements right was not enough and that specific training in group work behaviour may also be needed.

Commentary

The topic is obviously an important one and is of especial relevance to lecturers involved in vocationally oriented degrees, where employers' demands for the development of group working skills have considerable weight. The researchers succinctly identify common problems with group work, from their own experience and from the literature. The research report is well written, with clearly marked sections taking the reader through the issues and what was done. The data collected for the evaluation stage is clearly presented in tables and all conclusions are clearly warranted. The structured discussion data are triangulated with the questionnaire data.

There are some conspicuous gaps, nevertheless. We are not given any clue about the authors' approach to the ethical issues involved in researching as part of their teaching, nor are we apprised of the management of the relationship between the researchers and their colleagues. The authors make no reference to the methodological literature, making it harder for the reader to evaluate the research.

What did the research tell us about group work? The research offers credible evidence-based practical advice to lecturers employing group methods. The authors demonstrate the efficacy of a particular set of organisational procedures, and they demonstrate a way of accommodating students' preferences for individual or co-operative work. They also emphasise the importance of ongoing tutor support, particularly in making students aware of group processes, providing interim feedback and acting as an adjudicator where there is conflict (p. 79).

Case study 2

Solon, T. (2007) 'Generic Critical Thinking Infusion and Course Content Learning in Introductory Psychology'. Journal of Instructional Psychology 34, 2: 95–109

The question as to whether critical thinking can be explicitly taught and the learning acquired transferred to other subject areas in which students are primarily working has been hotly debated over many years. There have been disputes both about what is meant by 'critical thinking' and about what are the most appropriate pedagogical methods for teaching it. At one extreme lie those who believe that critical thinking is a discrete set of skills which can be applied with good effect to any subject matter whatsoever. It is not uncommon for those in this camp to believe that critical thinking skills have a very wide scope indeed, which includes, as well as the abilities to develop and understand arguments, the ability to compare, to solve problems, to evaluate, etc. (de Bono 1978, cited in Johnson 2010). Others hold that the ability to understand, criticise and develop arguments is to some extent common across different subjects and can be developed within the teaching of one subject matter in order to be applied across a range of other subjects (Siegel 2010). Others again are sceptical that there are any critical thinking skills independent of the subject matter in which they are exercised, and maintain that they are not transferable from one subject to another (e.g. McPeck 1990).

There is relatively little empirical evidence on the efficacy of teaching thinking skills. Solon (2007), who reviews the most significant of the existing literature, makes a significant claim. He conducted a quasi-experimental study that involved a group of students that he was himself teaching in which ten hours of the course was to be devoted to critical thinking. His intention was to determine whether a structured programme in teaching thinking skills could be effective within an undergraduate course without at the same time adversely affecting the learning of the content of that course. It was thus a small-scale study in which a group of psychology students of similar attainment were divided into two equal groups: control and experimental. The study was thus quasi-experimental and was not an RCT (randomised control trial) since there was no genuinely random way of selecting the sample for the experiment. One group was given the intervention, the other was taught without the intervention. The experimental group, however, was also given an infusion programme of generic critical thinking instruction and twenty hours extra homework based on the Toulmin argument model (Toulmin et al. 1984), while the control group was not. (An infusion programme is one that is carried out within the main programme of study rather than as a completely separate programme.) The approach to critical thinking thus adopted was close to that advocated by Siegel (2010) and concentrated on developing argumentative abilities.

The result of following the programme was that those in the experimental group made significant gains on the Cornell Z test as a measure of critical thinking compared with the control group. They did this without any detriment to their performance on a psychology test compared to the control group. The study thus appeared to provide evidence for the claim that pursuing a course of study in critical thinking within the context of a subject-based programme can be done successfully in the sense that improvements in critical thinking can result without any apparent losses in students' learning in their subject, in this case psychology. Solon acknowledges the limitations of a small-scale (not purely experimental) study and the need for further work, but suggests that this study shows that critical thinking can be taught through infusion methods without detriment to subject instruction.

Commentary

The Solon report is of a well-designed quasi-experimental study that reports statistically significant results for student achievement in critical thinking. The results presented here are very interesting, particularly in their report of non-detriment to the learning of the primary subject matter, which is obviously a concern whenever curriculum substitution is mooted. One may, however, wonder how to interpret these results as they relate to critical thinking ability. The experimental group received instruction in generic (transferable) critical thinking skills and the post-experimental critical thinking instrument, the Cornell Z test, measured ability in generic critical thinking. Thus it was established that instruction in generic critical thinking within the experimental group resulted in statistically significant increases in test scores in critical thinking skills. While significant, this result is not very surprising. It would have been surprising to have found no improvement in critical thinking skills in the intervention group, given that they received instruction in critical thinking and the control group did not. In this sense, the study does not necessarily tell us anything that is very interesting.

More interesting is that fact that the intervention group, although they received ten hours less instruction in psychology overall than the control group, did not seem to have lost out in terms of their learning of psychology. This suggests either that parts of the psychology teaching were not effective for the control group, or that there was some transfer effect from the teaching of critical thinking into the understanding of the psychology material. Neither of these propositions was tested within the study.

The claim for the teaching of thinking skills is usually that they are *transferable*. This means that the skills and knowledge acquired on such a programme can be profitably used on other programmes. Apart from the bare possibility mentioned above, that the grasp of critical thinking had a positive effect on the learning of psychology, there is no evidence of the transferability of critical thinking skills in the Solon study. Evidence that the teaching of critical thinking had a positive effect on the understanding of psychology would have been necessary in order for this claim to be made plausible. Most advocates of the teaching of critical thinking would, however, maintain that being transferable means that such abilities could be profitably employed in a range of subject matters once they had either been acquired separately or in the context of learning within another subject.

To show, as Solon appears to have done, that instruction in critical thinking improves one's abilities as a critical thinker, at least as measured by a test, is not however, sufficient to show that the critical thinking skills thus acquired were *transferable* to other subjects apart from, possibly, psychology. It would be necessary to conduct further empirical work in order to test this proposition, let alone to establish whether improved critical thinking abilities as measured on a test of critical thinking resulted in improved understanding and performance in a range of subject matters. Solon's study could thus be said to remove some of the ambiguities around the claims made about the efficacy of the teaching of critical thinking, namely the possibility that improvement in critical thinking is gained at the expense of subject knowledge. Of course, one cannot exclude the possibility that there is a particular relationship between psychology and critical thinking that does not apply to the latter's relationship with other subject matters. Solon's work illustrates the need to press on further with testing the transferability claim for critical thinking by testing what, if any, positive effects it has on the subsequent learning of students in other subject matters.

The Solon study does not contain any discussion of the ethics of this kind of intervention study and one should note that both groups were at potential risk: the intervention group from suffering in their learning of psychology, the control group in failing to learn any thinking skills.

Case study 3

Howell, D. (2009) 'Occupational Therapy Students in the Process of Interprofessional Collaborative Learning: A Grounded Theory Study'. Journal of Interprofessional Care 23, 1: 667–80

Interprofessional education for health professionals aims at enabling them to work together, and with other professionals such as social workers, to give a better service to patients or clients. The requirement for interprofessional education is relatively recent in the UK and it is an area that is arguably under-researched.

Howell's research draws on her experience of teaching interprofessional health education in the USA. The purpose of her study is to generate a theory of the learning process of occupational therapy students (OTs) engaged in collaborative learning with other students from a variety of other health professions, in order to help lecturers to devise better curricula.

Howell's study involved four sites where students were undertaking different collaborative activities. The data comprised semi-structured interviews with nine students about their experiences of collaboration, which Howell defines 'as a process in which two or more students in different allied health educational programs worked together to contribute to planning, decision making, and problem solving toward a mutual purpose or goal established in the course objectives' (Howell 2009: 69).

The interview data was analysed using the grounded theory approach (Strauss and Corbin 1998), and a software package was used to help with the organisation of the data. The findings were identified factors central to the OTs' process of interprofessional collaborative learning. According to Howell these were: 'holding your weight, representing the OT field, problem solving, working as a team, and learning'. These processes were essential to 'building a culture of mutual respect', a core emergent category (Howell 2009: 71).

The concern for mutual respect between allied health professionals as a factor in successful interprofessional education has been found in other studies. Howell argues, therefore, that this needs to be taken into account by lecturers who design curricula.

Howell found that there are various factors influencing 'respect'. For example some students had previous experience, which was thought to give them an advantage in the 'pecking order' of the group. Howell remarks that the influence of these factors on successful group collaboration needs further investigation. Furthermore the study suggested that OT students tended to have a weak professional identity and to feel undervalued by others in the health team. Howell suggests that it might be useful for lecturers who teach OT students to recognise that some may 'struggle with developing their professional identity', perhaps more than students from other areas. The study represents a 'first step' in understanding the process that OT students experience in interprofessional education, and more work needs to be undertaken, perhaps focusing on the experience of students in other professions.

Commentary

The report of the research is exemplary. The process of coding is explained and illustrated and the steps taken to verify interpretations are clearly described. The author constructed an audit trail, as recommended by Miles and Huberman (1994), which was checked by an external auditor during the final phase of analysis. Interpretations were triangulated with other sources of data obtained through observation and with the literature, and member checks were carried out. The ethics section describes steps taken to obtain institutional permission and informed consent from the students. The ethical problem of researching one's own students is briefly discussed.

What did the research tell us about interprofessional education? The research makes one strong claim and some weaker claims. The strong claim is that successful interprofessional working depends on mutual respect. Unlike the Parsons and Drew (1996) study, which looked at the problems inherent in the organisation and management of group working, Howell's study unearthed the emotional dynamics involved in working with others who have differential levels of expertise, different levels of experience and come from different disciplinary backgrounds. The research is important therefore in directing the attention of curriculum designers to a qualitatively different problem involved in group work. Howell's suggestion that OTs' sense of professional value be addressed is important and an interesting contribution to our knowledge of collaborative group working.

Case study 4

Hartsell, B. D. and Parker, A. J. (2008) 'Evaluation of Problem-Based Learning as a Method for Teaching Social Work Administration: A Content Analysis'. Administration in Social Work 32, 3: 44–62

The authors' focus is problem-based learning (PBL) in a social work administration class. PBL, sometimes called enquiry-based learning (EBL), is claimed to provide students with learning opportunities to develop insights and skills otherwise unavailable in more didactic approaches to teaching and learning (see e.g. Ashby et al. 2006). Hartsell agrees with this view. He argues that from his own experience, and anecdotal evidence, didactic teaching methods are suitable for teaching principles and concepts but are less effective in helping students apply their knowledge. His view is supported by a literature review, although a drawback of previous work in problem-based learning in social administration has been the absence of interaction with real clients. He designed his class so that his students worked with a group of homeless people who wished to constitute themselves as a formal organisation for the purposes of advocacy and grant funding. The first author is the teacher and researcher, the second a student in the class who took on the role of 'moderator'. The purpose of the study was to evaluate the effectiveness of PBL as an approach to teaching social work administration.

Hartsell and Parker use a definition of PBL and what it is intended to achieve following Barrows (2000). PBL is described as student-centred, utilising small groups facilitated or guided by the lecturer. The group works on a problem in order to develop relevant concepts and skills. New information is acquired by the students through their own research. The learning objectives are to acquire an integrated knowledge base structured around the problem, the learning of effective problem-solving approaches and the development of team skills. The work is to a large extent directed by the students.

The research participants were ten out of eleven students taking the PBL class. Their age range was from 24–54 years old. The course met for ten weeks between 6:00 and 10:00 p.m. In the first meeting the syllabus was given out, with the assessment requirements. One part of the assessment consisted of a report to the clients and another part consisted of a reflective essay. The research used the latter as the data for the research, subjecting them to a content analysis to gauge what had been learnt. Hartsell describes the process of content analysis that he and the student moderator carried out independently. After three phases of coding the authors derived seven themes which described what students had learnt. These were: ethics, administration concepts, myself, application versus theory, structure, challenging details, and internal conflict. Each theme is discussed and illustrated with quotations.

From this discussion several conclusions are drawn. The strategy of infusing the social work curriculum with ethics seemed to work. The authors also felt that students had become aware of ideas that they were previously unaware of and had a sense of what they needed to know. They had learnt about themselves and had engaged in a struggle to reconcile their professional obligation to show unconditional positive regard to their clients, with their feelings of disapproval of their unreliability due to alcoholism and other problems. They also appeared to have learnt the value of appropriate structures, competent leadership, the value of a supportive learning environment and the value of 'knowledge before action'.

Commentary

The research findings are couched in a very tentative way, reflecting the authors' awareness of problems with the conduct of the research. The unit of analysis of the essays was not agreed before content analysis took place, leading to some doubts about its rigour. The attempt to obtain a good measure of inter-coder reliability is described in some detail. Furthermore, because there is no comparison group or measure, the authors cannot be sure that the kind of learning they describe would not have taken place in a more traditional classroom. On a more positive note, the students did point to weaknesses in the pedagogical approach. For instance, some students pointed out that while they learnt about their part of the assignment, they learnt very little about the part assigned to other students, even though they had to produce a composite report. The author introduced modifications to future classes, so that there are fewer meetings with clients, and more opportunities for the students to share, formally, their discoveries. The research was valuable in that it allowed the author to make more informed choices in curriculum design.

Despite the limitations of the research methodology, the researchers felt that there was evidence to show that the students had a 'rich' learning experience. They would not wish to make any generalisations based on their findings, but recommend further research work be undertaken. From the qualitative work they carried out they suggest the following three hypotheses would be worthy of investigation: students in a class structured around problem-based learning learn more about ethics than students in traditional classes; students learn the connections between ideas and their application better through problem-based learning than through traditional learning methods; and students in traditional classes perform better on tests of content than students in classes that use problem-based learning.

Conclusion

These four case studies illustrate the potential of practitioner research to recommend strategies to 'solve' what otherwise might be regarded as intractable practice problems; to investigate complex but central pedagogical problems such as the transferability of generic skills; and to unearth feelings and emotions that lie beneath the surface.

References

Ashby, J., Hubbert, V., Cotrel-Gibbons, L., Cox, K., Digan, J., Lewis, K., Langmack, G., Matiti, M., McCormick, D., Roberts, L., Taylor, D., Thom, N., Wiggs, M. and Wilson, L. (2006) 'The Enquiry-based Learning Experience: An Evaluation Project'. *Nurse Education in Practice* 6, 22–30.

Barrows, H. S. (2000) Foreword. In D. H. Evensen and C. E. Hmelo (eds) *Problem-based Learning: A Research Perspective on Learning Interactions*. Mahwah, NJ: Lawrence Erlbaum.

de Bono, E. (1978) *Teaching Thinking*. Harmondsworth: Penguin.

Hartsell, B. D. and Parker, A. J. (2008) 'Evaluation of Problem-Based Learning as a Method for Teaching Social Work Administration: A Content Analysis'. *Administration in Social Work* 32, 3: 44–62.

Howell, D. (2009) 'Occupational Therapy Students in the Process of Interprofessional Collaborative Learning: A Grounded Theory Study'. *Journal of Interprofessional Care* 23, 1: 667–80.

Johnson, S. (2010) 'Teaching Thinking Skills', in C. Winch (ed.) *Teaching Thinking Skills*. London: Continum.

McPeck, J. E. (1990) *Teaching Critical Thinking*. New York: Routledge.

Miles, M. B. and Huberman, A. M. (1994) *Qualitative Data Analysis*. 2nd edn. Thousand Oaks, CA: Sage.

Parsons, D. E and Drew, S. K. (1996) 'Designing Group Project Work to Enhance Learning: Key Elements'. *Teaching in Higher Education* 1, 1: 65–80.

Siegel, H. (2010) 'On Thinking Skills', in C. Winch (ed.) *Teaching Thinking Skills*. London: Continuum.

Solon, T. (2007) 'Generic Critical Thinking Infusion and Course Content Learning in Introductory Psychology'. *Journal of Instructional Psychology* 34, 2: 95–109.

Strauss, A. and Corbin, J. (1998) *Basics of Qualitative Research: Techniques and Procedures for Developing Grounded Theory*. 2nd edn. Thousand Oaks, CA: Sage.

Toulmin, S., Rieke, R. and Janik, A. (1984) *An Introduction to Reasoning*. 2nd edn. New York: Macmillan.

Winch, C. (ed.) (2010) *Teaching Thinking Skills*. London: Continuum.

Glossary

Assessment of prior learning   a process whereby prior learning is accredited so that exemption from parts of a course can be granted. Where prior experiential learning experiences are accredited, it is called the Assessment of Prior Experiential Learning (APEL).

Audit trail   a document that records chronologically the data or evidence collected in a research project and the decisions taken with regard to its analysis. It may be a self-designed proforma or one taken from the research literature. The aim is maximum transparency so that an independent person can check that the steps taken have been valid.

Case   a bounded instance, such as a person, school or university. The study of cases involves the collection of mainly qualitative data, but can include quantitative data. We have recommended that a multimethod approach to studying cases be used.

Competency   the ability to carry out a task or operation effectively.

Constant comparative method   involves the comparison of qualitative data items (such as transcripts of interviews) in the search for emergent categories. Such categories are tested and refined by searching for exceptions which act as counter-examples and thus check the development of false theories. The method is associated with grounded theory and the work of Glaser and Strauss.

Data   the record of observations made during research. Data can be numerical, or they can consist of spoken words, text, diagrams, pictures, artefacts or film. The word 'data' is sometimes used to refer to quantitative data only, and the word 'evidence' to qualitative data only, but often the words are used, as we have done, interchangeably.

Empirical
an adjective meaning 'related to experience, especially sensory experience'. A method, statement or belief is said to be empirical if it is derived from, or has a basis in direct observation.

Epistemology
a branch of philosophical inquiry that focuses on the nature and possibility of knowledge. It is concerned with how knowledge is acquired, held and what its scope and limits are. Epistemologists are concerned with the meanings of related concepts, such as evidence, proof, certainty, belief, memory and perception.

Evidence
facts, whose occurrence supports a claim. Primary evidence consists of the original facts that support the claim. Secondary evidence consists of traces derived from primary evidence. The term 'evidence' is sometimes used to refer to qualitative data as opposed to quantitative data. See entry for 'data' above.

Fixed designs
A fixed research design is one that is 'fixed', i.e. the research questions are decided before data collection begins. For example a survey questionnaire is designed before data collection, although some previous research (piloting) will usually have been carried out before it is 'fixed'. Fixed designs are generally quantitative. The contrast is with flexible designs where the research questions can be modified, after a period of data collection and analysis, and/ or the selection of respondents may change depending on the findings that are emerging.

Flexible designs
A flexible design may allow for the change either of the research questions or research respondents or sites as the research develops. This approach is primarily qualitative although it can include quantitative data. The contrast is with fixed designs. See entry for 'fixed designs' above.

Generalisability
refers to that aspect of research which allows findings or recommendations to be applied to other populations or contexts. The characteristics of a generalisation differs according to the design and presuppositions of the research.

Grounded theory a systematic approach to qualitative data collection and analysis that aims to discover (rather than impose) theoretical constructs.

Hypothesis a conjecture or supposition. A hypothesis may be used to predict the likely outcome of an intervention, or as a way of organising the collection of data.

Ideology sets of ideas associated with political, social or religious presuppositions.

Inductive an inference from a limited number of particular cases to further cases, future events or a general conclusion. For example, from observing that all swans are white in my experience, I may argue inductively that the next swan I see will be white, or that all swans are white.

Insider someone who works or otherwise belongs in a setting that they are researching. Practitioners are insiders in this respect.

Member checking the procedure whereby interpretations of respondents' words or ideas are checked with them either for their accuracy or for their views on the researcher's interpretation.

Methodology the thinking behind the use of methods chosen. This may extend to philosophical views of reality and the nature of knowledge.

Multimethods the use of qualitative and quantitative research methods.

Nomological pertaining to a law of nature. Nomological explanations make use of the concepts of cause and effect.

Normative governed by rules or standards. Explanations are given in terms of rules, standards and reasons for action.

Null hypothesis A hypothesis is a conjecture or supposition, which may be subjected to investigation. For example it could be hypothesised that 'training in group work methods will lead to better learning outcomes'. The null hypothesis states the opposite, that training in group work methods has no effect on the quality of learning outcomes.

Objective   If someone is objective it implies that they are unbiased or non-partisan in their opinions. To refer to an objective state of affairs, on the other hand, usually means there are facts and situations in the world that exist independently of anyone's awareness of them.

Ontology   a theory or theories of being or the nature of existence.

Phronesis   wisdom or good judgement.

Positivist   Positivist theories of knowledge claim that all knowledge is based, ultimately, on sense experience. An assumption of positivism is that reality exists independently of people's perceptions and that it is governed by laws which can be discovered using experimental methods.

Randomised controlled trial (RCT)   a research design in which the participants are randomly allocated to either an experimental group or a control group. The experimental group receives an intervention, the control group does not. From a comparison between the outcomes from the two groups, inferences are made about the effect of the intervention.

Realist   someone who holds the view that a reality exists independently of our thinking or feeling. An implication of this view is that entities can be discovered.

Reliability   refers to the idea that if the research were repeated then the results would be the same, increasing our confidence in the validity of the results. The idea is well developed in quantitative research but is less easily applied to qualitative research.

Research   The Higher Education Funding Council for England (HEFCE) has defined research as 'original investigation in order to gain knowledge and understanding'. It includes work of direct relevance to the needs of commerce and industry, as well as to the public and voluntary sectors and scholarship (including pedagogic research); the invention and generation of ideas, images, performances and artefacts including design, where these lead to new or substantially improved insights; and the use of existing knowledge in experimental development to produce new or substantially improved materials, devices, products and processes, including design and construction. It excludes routine testing and analysis of materials, components and processes, e.g. for the maintenance of national standards, as distinct from the development of new analytical techniques. It also excludes the development of teaching materials that do not embody original research. Scholarship is the 'creation, development and maintenance of the intellectual infrastructure of subjects and disciplines' (HEFCE: RAE definition of research, 2006).

Sampling   In qualitative research sampling (choosing who or what to study from a total population) is usually purposive, that is, it is dictated by the research questions and conceptual framework. The sample (people, settings, events or processes) may change as the research develops in the way that a detective follows up clues. For example, if I am interested in what counts as good history writing, I may begin by interviewing history teachers and then find it necessary to interview the chief examiners of examination boards, and university lecturers. Alternatively sampling can be random. This means that the sample chosen is believed to be representative of the wider population of which it is a part. For example if I chose a certain kind of pear for its taste, I assume that all the other pears of that name will have the same taste. To make a random selection requires a sampling frame such as a list of all relevant people or objects. To revert to our previous example, if I were to carry out a random survey of students' views of history writing I might use a list of all history A-level candidates for a certain year and select names out of a hat.

Scepticism   Philosophical scepticism involves doubting that anything can be known in a certain area. More generally scepticism means an approach to critical thinking that involves doubting the truth of what is claimed as a way of examining its relative strength and/or merit.

Scholarship   See the entry for research above.

Standards   A standard is a yardstick against which something may be measured or compared. For example a size 8 shoe will be of a standardised length. Judgements of value can enter into standards, for instance a 5-star hotel will have certain desirable qualities. The standards in research are judged by the qualities that research ought to have. These qualities may be contested.

Subjective
This term can refer to a person's views or preferences that are her own and are possibly not shared by others. For example her view that frogs are cute is a subjective view, which is neither true nor false. In another sense, some experiences can be subjective, in that they are known introspectively, as for instance a pain, or an emotion. To criticise a view as merely subjective is to use the first meaning of the word and to imply that it is, in a sense, arbitrary. Objectivity, on the other hand, implies that the element of personal preference or viewpoint has been eliminated.

Task and achievement concepts
This is a distinction introduced by G. Ryle in *The Concept of Mind*. A task word is one that refers to a task that is ongoing, e.g. 'looking'. An achievement word is one that refers to the completion of a task, e.g. 'found'. The same word may have a 'task' and an 'achievement' sense, for example, 'learning', or 'teaching'. The distinction is useful in clarifying when a word is being used in which sense, and can help to clear up conceptual confusion.

Triangulation
To triangulate means to check the accuracy of a participant's viewpoint or a theory by seeking corroboration from other sources of data, produced by different methods. For example, interview data may be compared with documentary evidence or observations. Positive corroboration increases confidence in the validity of one's interpretation of the data.

Validity
refers to the epistemological status of research findings or recommendations. If research is valid, we know that the researchers have taken steps to minimise possible objections to the correctness of claims made. The degree to which research findings or recommendations are valid is important for decision making. Approaches to establishing the validity of research differ depending on the design.

Index

accountability 1; professionally accountable 11, 86; *see also* UK Professional Standards Framework for Teaching and Supporting Learning in Higher Education

action research: action research/action learning distinction 13, 91; action research case study 13, 32, 39–40, 82, 83–88 (action 83–84; critical friends 87, 107; insiders/outsiders: ethical matters 86–87; Parsons, D. and Drew, S. 39–40, 73, 104, 130; problem, research question 39, 84, 86, 87–88, 91, 105; reports 41; steps 39, 87–88, 105–7; validity 104, 105–7; validity, threats to 105, 106, 107; who defines the problem? 84–85; working with others: collaboration/cooperation 36, 39, 85–86, 106); compulsory education 17; data 87, 106; democratic spirit 84, 86; Elliott, J. 88, 89; evidence-based practice in British education 16–19; models 13; participants 32, 84–85, 90, 118 (quality of relationships 104, 106); partnership work 39, 85–86; practitioner research 16–17; reflective practice/action research differences 5, 13; theory 84, 85; versions 88–91 (action research as critical social science 84, 90–91; action research as practical philosophy 84, 88–89; technical action research 40, 84, 89–90, 123–24); *see also* case study; Parsons, D. and Drew, S.; practitioner research, models

acts, laws, agreements: Data Protection Act (1998) 114, 119; Education Act (1988) 17; Education Act (1992) 17; Education Reform Act (2004) 1 (National Student Survey (2004–9) 1)

argument, argumentation 21, 58; claims/evidence, argumentation 29, 41, 45, 57, 58, 79, 134; evaluation 58; inductive 45; replicability 58; *see also* evidence; research: reading and evaluation

assessment 3, 42; assessment of prior experiential learning (APEL) 133; assessment of prior learning (APL) 11, 33, 133; compulsory education 17; enhancing the quality of assessment: the case of dissertations in sociology 77–79; evaluation/assessment distinction 93; evidence 74; formative assessment 74; group work 9, 39, 69, 104, 123–26, 130; higher education 17; national assessment 17, 25; pedagogy and assessment 28; summative assessment 74; using assessment as method for collecting data 74–75; *see also* evaluation

audit trail 58, 66–67, 74, 97, 129, 133; *see also* data; evidence; quality

bias 18, 98, 100; member checking 103, 135; researcher bias 103; *see also* validity

British Education Research Association, *Ethical Guidelines* (BERA) 84–85, 114–16; confidentiality and anonymity 120; deception, subterfuge 116; ethic of respect for persons 115; ethics of collaboration 119; participant 115 (informed